super
SALESMANSHIP

+

convincing
ADVERTISING

=

lucrative
BUSINESS

JOHN MEPHAM

IBSN: 13:978-1496042750
Copyright @ 2014 John Mepham
All rights reserved

ABOUT THE AUTHOR

I joined a firm of estate agents and auctioneers when leaving school. After gaining valuable experience in the property business I became a partner in a well-established firm of estate agents.

My connections with certain business associates led to me being offered the position of Managing Director of a public property company with a quote on the London Stock Exchange. Being always willing to go the next step up the career ladder I willingly accepted. I held that post for some twenty-two years.

Until my retirement I was a Chartered Surveyor.

During all my years in the tough property world I have negotiated at the highest level and drafted hundreds of advertisements that successfully did their job. Therefore, without doubt, I have the experience and knowledge to put this book before you.

JOHN MEPHAM

CONTENTS

THE OBJECTIVES OF THIS BOOK

In every profession, business and trade there are differing types of expertise that are helping the enterprise to prosper. Owners and/or their managers have the skills to bring those differing strands together to produce a well-run and profitable concern. Consider a range of successful businesses and endeavour to ascertain the various skills needed to bring success. When considering each specific business it will become apparent that two special skills are a prerequisite to success. Those skills are **SALESMANSHIP AND ADVERTISING**. Contemplate, just for a moment, the type of business that prospers without those skills. That exercise will convince you that both salesmanship and advertising cover a wide range of activities and are present in commerce in many different ways.

After an outlay of valuable capital a manufacturer has goods to sell. There is no alternative those goods MUST be sold; that is where salesmanship and advertising come to the fore. Only by super use of those two skills will the goods be sold at a satisfactory price. The goods enter a supply chain right down to the consumer. Therefore, there may be many salespersons and advertisers within that supply chain. So, the manufacturer would be relying on that expertise - there is no doubt whatsoever about that.

The predicament is now with the salesperson who must display the goods before middlemen and/or the public. The more people who know that the goods are available for sale the greater the chance of success. The purchasers know where goods needed are for sale as advertising is carried out in many different ways and is the salesperson's main tool of his trade

SALESMANSHIP must be used when disposing of all goods and services

SALESMANSHIP entails ADVERTISING

...as the song says, "You can't have one without the other".

A WARNING –
TECHNOLOGY WON`T SAVE YOU

Nowadays when you enter an office it looks like a very clean well-ordered light industrial unit. It looks remarkably efficient. Every gleaning and up-to-date piece of equipment is ready to go...but, to where? Without the trained personnel all those sophisticated pieces of expensive equipment are just...pieces of expensive equipment. The vital ingredient to get things moving is the personnel of the firm.

All those appliances are the tools, not the masters, of success. Without a human being - that is you and me - the machinery would not start. Even today and for many future days the personal element in most activities will continue to be the controlling factor.

The message is plain and simple, yet so crucial to your future success. Be the master of all that equipment. Never for one moment forget that you are the human element that profits from their very existence. Wisely use them. However, do not drift away from all the personal traits that are still vitally necessary to give you both a successful career and a good life outside of the working environment.

TECHNOLOGY IS A SUPER AID –
NO MORE, NO LESS

ON SALESMANSHIP

1

IT ALL DEPENDS ON YOU

My personal motto has always been **NOTHING HAPPENS UNLESS YOU MAKE IT.** Read it again. It is relevant in all walks of life. As an example, when you sell goods or services unless you have the enterprise to start you will not succeed. In fact, you will not even start! To sit and think about selling - well, that is a fine and pleasant thought, but sooner or later action must start. With my personal motto in mind start now. Learn to sell and advertise in a more skilled, professional and profitable manner. Then, you will really be making something happen that will benefit your career and your life generally.

What do you consider to be the most important and precious asset that you have to sell? Think hard...you have it! It is yourself - **YOU.** Yes, you are constantly selling yourself. Now, that is truly significant. When performing any action and/or talking you are nearly always putting yourself on show. Hence, you are likely to get a reaction from some other person/s. You are the actor and there is the audience looking and listening to all that you say. You see, you must constantly "sell yourself" so as to be acceptable to all those who look and listen. Of course, most of the time you are not conscious of selling yourself. It comes naturally; it is a direct result of your upbringing plus your learning from personal experiences. Nevertheless, there are specific occasions when it is imperative that a correct image is projected. You must teach yourself to project that necessary attribute. This applies when you are working and meeting other persons. It applies even more when you are negotiating. It must not be forgotten that you sell yourself in everyday life when you are not working. Here are a few examples - being interview for a new job, taking a driving test, talking to a neighbour about some trees that are dangerously overhanging the driveway to your garage, having the first meeting with your future mother-in-law, et al.

Robert Louis Stevenson wisely said, "Everybody lives by selling something". Make a careful note of that quotation. It is so true and underlines the message of this book. That "something" may well be in both your working and non-working life.

It must be admitted that some persons have a natural charm and "sell themselves" without any effort whatsoever. Lucky people! That last remark must not depress you as the majority of the population do not possess that natural charm. Often quite the reverse. You are probably average, somewhere between the two extremes. Therefore, you are in front of many persons who have little or no charm and that is a fine start.

It is not an easy task to define, even in your own private thoughts, "natural charm". The essential pre-requisite that sets the scene to so many situations. It is being captivating, likeable, irresistible, friendly...it is being that someone whom others are comfortable being with and enjoy that relationship. When you have acquired those desired results you have nearly found the answer.

To summarise –

(1) You must not be content to just sell goods or services.
You must never forget that, at the same time, you are always selling yourself.

(2) You must not leave your charm in the workplace. You must take it into your home, your hobbies, your sport and so on

(3)   Always remember - **NOTHING HAPPENS UNLESS YOU MAKE IT** - applies in all walks of life

2

JUST A LITTLE THEORY

"Oh dear, not boring theory", I hear you mutter. I agree theory can be boring and too academic. You may be one of the majority who think, "Let`s get on with real life and leave the theory to academics who have the time to sit and think". That is fair comment but a little theory gives a perfect base on which to build a secure career that involves both salesmanship and advertising. Look at it this way. The best built house will soon totter into disrepair if constructed on faulty foundations. The houses that stand the test of time are those where the architect and the structural engineer have used their expertise to make sure that the foundations will take the weight of the houses built thereon. You will, of course, realise the importance of that analogy. So, please, read this chapter carefully. Get the foundations right and create a worthwhile career and private life.

So, a little theory that touches and concerns both salesmanship and advertising is advantageous. The main purpose of this book is to give helpful tips which can **immediately** be put into your everyday life/work routines. That is taking theory and using it profitably. We will waste not a second of valuable time waffling on about pointless and profitless theory. A useful slogan - he who waffles loses the deal.

When discussing theory it is useful to give examples relating to everyday and not get lost in a fog of intellectual claptrap. In this chapter are suggestions that must not be overlooked. My idea of the only way to use theory is to relate it to the real tough world of wheeler-dealing.

A very important question - what makes a first-class salesperson/negotiator? In a sentence the simple answer is one who again and again wins over the competitor. That is, however, the **result** of being a success. That end result illustrates that the person does it alone. So, it is **YOU** - and **YOU** alone - against the rest. The first requisite must be you. A really good salesperson is clear that it all depend on him. To put it so that my readers clearly realise the message - only you can fight and win your own battles. Like boxers in the ring, the seconds are out and each boxer is on his own.

To become a person who stands out from the crowd you must (1) be enthusiastic for your job (2) be enthusiastic about the goods or services being sold (3) be enthusiastic and know all about the workings of the firm that employs you (4) be an opportunist (5) be calm and never lose your temper (6) never boast (7) always be or appear to be both a reasonable and genuinely cheerful person (8) never be argumentative (9) never be greedy.

The above nine attributes will be discussed in other parts of this book. Nevertheless, here is the start of your quest to improve. How many of those guiding lights disclose any shortcomings in your salesmanship? Here is an opportunity to jump straight from theory into action. Use those guides to help improvements that will immediately benefit you. Take those guides that show a fault in your make-up into the marketplace today and see how their correction will benefit your sale figures. Be a little patient - it takes time to cure most things.

To succeed you must be a person whom others like to meet, who is a decent sort of chap and not one who seeks to win at **all** costs. That is the face that you must present to the business world. In the final analysis the foundation of your successful life and career is the face you present to all those whom you meet. Pull the wrong face and it will be much harder to ride the "slings and arrows of outrageous fortune." It is vital to remember that if you show faith in an individual you could well be rewarded by his faith in you.

Do not wait to become that decent chap. Start today - again it is up to you. No one will help you; it is just you alone. It depends on your correct personal qualities - read again those nine attributes listed above. Get that right and the job of selling becomes somewhat easier. Get the correct outlook and never forget that at all times you are additionally selling yourself.

Looking again at that intriguing question - what makes a first-class salesperson/negotiator? He must apply temperate persuasion, the gentle art of painlessly twisting arms and entering earnest and serious discussions in an attempt to win what he is seeking. Never being a bully, a liar or in any way being a conman. I like the phrase - one who sells has to calmly and ceaselessly explain. If you act professionally and sensibly your competitors will have no reason to dislike you. That will make it so much easier to strike a deal.

The two personal qualities that make a good salesperson are **ENTHUSIASM** and **CONFIDENCE.** Without both you will remain on the lower rungs of the ladder and never reach the top. Therefore, it is desirable to take a close look at both of these personalities. Here is yet another opportunity to mix theory with practice.

ENTHUSIASM - Enthusiasts are by their very nature fighters in so far as enthusiasm gives the strength and courage to push on as fast as possible towards the goal. It is behind all progress and betterment. Without it a weak desire withers and the target disappears into the distance and rarely reappears. The chance to achieve the target may never occur again. That is one of the sad facts of life, it is so easy to look back and sigh, "If only..."

But, beware. A word of warning is needed. Enthusiasm must not be a vehicle used to aim at the impossible. It must not lead to a wishy-washy fantasy. It must be a real desire for both a solid and responsible objective. Do not waste time and energy on daydreams.

Enthusiasm will clearly show that you have great confidence in your goods and services. It will say, "Deal with me for I know...yes, I really know...that you will be more than happy with my offerings". It is contagious; pass it on to your competitors. Then, your negotiations with them will be easier.

Your enthusiasm can and must be used to help others. This applies in work and in life generally. Be enthusiastic when asked for help or assistance. Give it freely and not in a half-hearted manner. Certainly, when negotiating such help will gain respect and you will be well on the way to a happy conclusion.

There is no doubt the enthusiasm will get you noticed and that is an immense plus. Very few persons are really enthusiastic. The true ones shine like a bright and vivid star that puts all the other stars to shame. It is fine low cost publicity and that, in itself, is a worthwhile achievement.

Enthusiasm has two vital components. Firstly, it has the same effect as perpetual motion - it keeps going. Once it is possessed it will keep you on your toes and increase your appetite to succeed. That must be an asset in life generally and more so when at work and negotiating. Secondly, it will spill over to others and you are likely to benefit from their additional interest and attention. Those are two useful advantages which must not be overlooked.

CONFIDENCE – If you are confident that your aim will be achieved you are on the way to that achievement. If you lack confidence - well, that is it, you are unlikely to succeed. Enthusiasm and confidence are, to a certain extent, linked; with both you are on to a winner. In fact if you lack the will to succeed you do not deserve to succeed.

Every now and then you will not feel enthusiastic and/or confident. Do not be too concerned. It happens to us all. We cannot be go-ahead and cheerful all the time. Generally there is a reason for that blow to your morale. Possibly you have just received a set-back that you cannot or will not accept. There are many reasons for that gloomy "It`s the end" feeling. You have no alternative; you must ride out the storm. Never let your predicament be visual. Keep it to yourself. This applies particularly when you are negotiating. You must take on the role of the actor and act as one who is both enthusiastic and confident. It will be difficult but it must be done. To smile and act cheerfully will not only help to conceal your dilemmas from others, it will have the beneficial effect of helping you to lose the blues. One action; two benefits. A useful suggestion - other persons like to know of your problems so that they can benefit there from - or just gloat. Few want to help you solve them. That is another reason why you must keep all those gloomy episodes to yourself.

To reach a goal you must think right and picture the fruits of winning. Think yourself towards success and you will surely succeed. In other words, think "confidence" and see that winning post. OK, that may sound very much like witchcraft. Do not take my word for it. Try it.

Behind the real show of confidence is the ability possessed to correctly do the job in hand. You must realise that you will not possess and display **REAL** confidence unless you have complete faith in your own ability. As an example, your aim is to score the winning goal in an important game of football. You are confident that it can be achieved as all the hard training over many weeks and the playing of some tough games have made you into both a fit and skilful player. Another example, you are a property negotiator showing a prospective buyer over a house. He stands in the hallway and seems very impressed. His wife even more so. You have trained hard to be a successful negotiator and realise that another sale is nearly in the bag. That inbuilt confidence will greatly assist in concluding a sale.

Confidence - the power house that will bring success is only provided by your own efforts. There is no safety net; no help from others. It is entirely in your own hands. This was brilliantly stated by President Abraham Lincoln, "Your own resolution to succeed is more important than any other thing". That quote from that esteemed person reinforces the advice given in many parts of this book.

You will now realise the valuable part played by both enthusiasm and confidence in salesmanship and in life generally as you consider synonyms of these two words:

ENTHUSIASM - passion, keenness, earnestness, eagerness, excitement, fervour, interest and zeal.

CONFIDENCE - assurance, self-reliance, trust, dependence and boldness.

To summarise - having both enthusiasm and confidence are the two main assets that form the basis of a good working and non-working life. Without them do not even think of being successful in the wide world of salesmanship. You will never reach your true potential.

ENTHUSIASM is the desire to win at all (reasonable) cost.

CONFIDENCE is knowing that both your ability and enthusiasm will see you prosper.

In life there is always the exception. There is, also, a qualification to the views expressed in the last few paragraphs. Imagine this scenario - it is January and a desolate cold and wet day in Brighton. You have a throbbing headache and are totally miserable. Nothing seems right. There is a crucial meeting in half-an-hour. If it is a success your career will bound ahead. If not...well...that is all too depressing to contemplate. There is no option - you must go to the meeting. This is one of those occasions when you become an actor. "You act as if..." You have to force yourself to talk and to act enthusiastically and confidently. That will be difficult but it must be done. The actor in you will hide the reality that you lack all positive feelings. All is not lost. In fact, as you act you will gain real enthusiasm and confidence - and the medicine will dull your headache! Do not forget that advice when the inevitable very bad day hits you.

A useful reminder - a false image will very soon be detected. When acting that is not really a worry for you will soon feel the returning glow of self-assurance. A totally false image is one of true deception. For example, trying to act as a top flight dealer when, as you well know, you are at best just a goodish one. Never try to act above your true self. It will not work. You will not even be fooling yourself and, being untrue to yourself, you will feel and look very uncomfortable.

PERSISTENCE - You have enthusiasm and confidence, that is fine. You must now add to those two valuable assets. That addition is persistence. There is little that is able to take the place of being truly persistent. There are very many ineffective and unsuccessful persons of real talent, even genius, who have failed through not being persistent. They would not persist and, in the main, gave up and moved on to an easier task. Many persons have little or no ambition and are very happy to have an average lifestyle. If that is their wish, fine. It is vital for you to know that you will not rise above the crowd unless you persist. Those who are capable of rising above the average and, yet, do not do so are generally guilty of not persisting. Some have reached a safe plateau in their careers and will not push (persist) for a more glittering position. The extra push could well have elevated them from above average success to being very successful. Maybe, by concentrating on their everyday work all ambition has been forgotten. That is an example that proves that you must be extremely tough and always persisting to reach the top of the business tree.

A useful suggestion - do not let the pressures of today remove ambition from your work agenda. So, to become a first-class negotiator you must persist - you must learn from each negotiation, you must seek new negotiating ideas, you must never relax (at work) and fall back on bad negotiating habits, you must keep moving forward...you must persist.

The slogan "persist, persist, persist" has a dynamic sound to it. Persistence will solve many problems, particularly when haggling. It has been the base on which many fine giant businesses were built. Someone persisted to get the enterprise started and to keep it going through both good and (very) bad times. Without persistence how many of today's well-known businesses would have failed? That is a thought that proves that persistence well and truly works.

A word of warning is as useful as a beneficial tip. Here is another one. How much time should be spent on trying? Time is a vital commodity, it must not be wasted. To keep trying when there is little hope of success is pointless. It is all very well saying - try, try and try again. It is repeated - to keep trying when you are convinced that there is no hope of success is utterly pointless. Experience will tell you when to throw in the towel. A useful suggestion - keep trying all the time that you **really** feel that it is worthwhile. When you get that feeling, "OK...one more try...just in case" you know that it is time to quit. Then, save time, money and energy. As is said, there is nothing to be gained by flogging a dead horse. What is the point?

Is it being proved to you that theory is not dull and as banal as you first thought? It is never easy or straightforward to discuss any theory without wandering off into useful practical applications. Hence, this chapter is giving you more suggestions, tips and ideas than you thought were possible. Just a little theory is giving you reasons for action.

You are now fully aware that every salesperson/negotiator that is good at his trade must be enthusiastic, confident and persistent, act in a calm and sensible manner and have the right personal qualities. I will speculate that you are thinking that it all seems a tall order and you will never succeed. OK, it is a tall order. Equally so, in respect that you will not succeed you could not be more wrong. You would not have purchased this book if there had not been just a little enthusiasm to progress. Do realise that you are already moving in the right direction. A useful reminder - nothing succeeds like success. That is a lesson that you are learning. Keep going - persist - persist - persist. Oscar Wilde said, "Nothing exceeds like excess". A wonderful Wildean epigram. Well, try for a little of that excess.

Once again the question is posed - what makes a first-class salesperson/negotiator? So many persons veer away from giving an answer and many sneer at him as a bad example of a "get rich at any price crook". That being so, it is necessary to explain to such persons that a salesperson/negotiator has a vital role to play in the economic scene. Without him the rate of sales in the economy as a whole would fall. So, of course, everyone would suffer. The manufacturer, the supplier of all those components, the wholesales, the retailer...the result being that wages across the entire economy would fall and there could well be a recession. Tell that to a detractor who attempts to mock and laugh at a car salesperson or a property negotiator, et al. Your attention is drawn to this myth as you may feel that your job is not one to boast about. Do not take that attitude. Tell the detractors that virtually all professions, businesses and trades rely on sales; hence, they rely on their sales team. What a glum, slow-moving and non-enterprising world it would be without salespersons and negotiators. Be firm and tell them that salespersons create sales, create wealth, create jobs and good wages for a majority of the population. There is more to it than that. You know it to be so and that gives you confidence in your own job and your future. It helps to make you an excellent dealer. So, hold your head up high and proudly go about your business.

Good negotiating is reasoning. It is not arguing in the sense that the scene is one of verbal battle often bordering on a blazing row. Reasoning can be usefully defined as arguing with all the rough edges smoothed away. Furthermore, when reasoning you are using all the facts and figures of your trade. You are not trying to bully your competitor into a deal. You are saying in a calm and quiet manner, "Listen, this must be right. All the info I have given you is true. Don`t you agree?" You pause and there is no response. You continue, "OK, I am wrong". That is sure to get a reply. That is an example of rational arguing. It involves moderation, sanity, sensible conduct and putting the case so that it is clearly understood and persuading the competitor to answer. That last proviso is the key - giving him the chance to answer. It will call to his attention that you are endeavouring to see all sides of the matter - even his.

A useful suggestion - selling is always reason based on reason based on reason...until the desired result is achieved.

Few people realise that nothing happens until you make it. It must be said that a limited number of happenings do take place against that assumption. These are generally not the good things in life. Almost always you have to do something to make a good occurrence happen. That is why it is imperative to take my motto into the business world. Therefore, as it is so important it is repeated - **NOTHING HAPPENS UNLESS YOU MAKE IT.**

As a simple example of that motto in action. You have seen a car for sale at £15,000. Of course, you could buy at that price. Being an optimist and believing my motto you decide to have a go. You offer £12,000. Your action paid off and a deal was done at £12,500. You see, you made something happen - you bought the car and saved £2,500. That was a good deal. You can clearly see the lesson of that simple example. You made something happen and you profited from that action. That illustrates another essential aspect of salesmanship. You made something happen **to your own advantage.** A useful reminder - your actions bring profits, you profit from your actions.

Did you notice that in the last paragraph four words were highlighted - **to your own advantage?** That four word group so very clearly illustrates what salesmanship is all about. It is concluding a deal on the terms that you required. You may well think that that is common sense. Of course it is - but it is very often overlooked. You are always trying to better the terms on offer to you. All that you say and do must have that objective in mind. Keep that constantly before you as you negotiate; that is the sole purpose of the exercise.

There is an old chestnut that has become stereotyped and is an integral part of all very poor negotiator's ammunition. It is that if you meet the competitor halfway between his price and yours a satisfactory deal has been concluded. In my view this split-the-difference ploy is seldom true negotiating. It is so often used by a lazy and/or defeated person. However, it can be successfully used when your efforts have nearly succeeded and you have the best acceptable terms from the competitor, yet you feel they may be bettered by putting a gun at his head - that is, by trying to split-the - difference. However, only use it in the following circumstances. You have narrowed the gap and you are prepared to risk a gamble. Your original target has been exceeded and, hence, you would be happy to close; but, you are feeling lucky, and try to split-the-difference. You may win that little extra or you may not, but remember this word of warning. The competitor may not like your tactics and may walk away. Whether or not to push for that extra is in your hands and the circumstances of each negotiation will help you to decide whether to close or to trust your luck. However, always keep in mind that it is often better not to be too greedy.

Here is an example of the circumstances mentioned in the last paragraph. You want to buy a load of scrap metal. It is on offer at £20,000. To you it is worth £17,500. You offer £15,000 and slowly and reluctantly the owner comes down to £18,000. It is nearly stalemate. The owner was prepared to accept £500 **more** than it is worth to you and says that is his lowest price. Here is an ideal situation to try a split-the-difference ploy. You put forward the middle price bid of £16,500. You have another £1,000 up your sleeve. A useful reminder - it is best not to use this ploy until your price objective has been achieved or very close to being achieved. Also, as in this example, if possible keep the middle price bid below your target price. You will then have a little more in your armoury as a final, final bid. That is super negotiating.

In this chapter the question posed - what makes a good salesperson/negotiator - has been answered. To be totally honest it has been answered as best as one can answer a conundrum. Also considered are some of the thoughts that a good salesperson should ponder and either put into action or in the bin. That has all helped to answer that difficult conundrum. You will realise that that is not enough. In real life you do not just sit and think. You have to act and get results - unless you want to starve. For that reason we now leave this theory chapter. That does not mean that you can forget its contents, quite the reverse. You should never forget or overlook those basic yet useful theories on salesmanship and negotiating.

A last reminder - all the theory in the world will only be of limited use if you ignore everyday experiences and do not profit from real happenings. There is a marvellous Aesop fable which illustrates that the events of today can help you to avoid the same blunders tomorrow. A dog went into a butcher's shop and seized a heart. The dog ran off. The butcher saw him running away and shouted, "I'll know you in future whenever I see you. I haven't lost a heart, I`ve learnt a lesson by heart". That is a useful reminder that you learn from day-to-day events...from experience.

3

INTO ACTION - THE ESSENTIALS

In this chapter the essentials that are needed to secure a win are set out. When considering these essentials remember that not all negotiations take place along the same lines. There will be twists and turns, high points, low points, sudden shocks, sudden pleasant surprises...nevertheless, with a firm grasp of these essentials you will be able to take all that is throw at you and bring the negotiations back into your favour. That will help you to think quickly on your feet and you will not be afraid of changing course. You will soon lose that feeling of being hidebound and restricted by convention.

To the novice both salesmanship and negotiating can be frightening. This applies, also, to the expert when sales are flagging. All the work put into your job could be time wasted if you cannot constantly sell your firms goods. You will be sacked and that`s that. A new start; a new struggle...it doesn`t bear thinking about. The prerequisite to success is that you must know inside out the goods or services you are endeavouring to sell. For example, what makes them unique to you? That is the kernel of your selling strategy. Maybe, uniqueness is found in design?...in their use?...in their price? To know all about your wares or services is the only way to real success. A useful suggestion - if you are not one hundred-per-cent au fait with your offerings to the public stop, think, take action and make sure that you are before starting your sales campaign.

THE FOUR PRIME ESSENTIALS ARE:
1 Know exactly what you want
2 Know, as far as is possible, what the competitor wants
3 Build-up your case to reflect (1) and (2)
4 Close the deal before it goes away

1 KNOW EXACTLY WHAT YOU WANT

"A mighty maze! But, not without a plan", wrote Alexander Pope. Without a plan you are as likely to get lost when negotiating as you are in that splendid maze at Hampton Court. The most concise plan will clearly display how to reach your target. It is not an iota of good facing a competitor and thinking; for example, if he will sell the car for £21,000 I may possibly buy it. That is a vague desire and is wishy-washy. It does not show a strong yearning that you really want the car at the lowest possible price. You must have a clear and firm target - that is, say, to buy at no more £19,000. That is a real sound desire; you have an objective firmly in mind. You will not be detracted from a successful conclusion on your terms. If you are unable to buy at or below your target figure you walk away.

In fact, you must go further than that suggested in the last paragraph. You are going to succeed; to cogitate otherwise will mean that the battle is as good as lost. Do not underrate your own capabilities. Your training and all the experience from past negotiations have given you that positive outlook. Walk into the negotiating chamber with a true confidence knowing exactly what you desire. You are more than an optimist, you are a realist and do not deal in hope value. You only deal in winning.

There is little to be gained in taking the attitude that you will do your best. Dismiss, "I always do my best" from your thoughts...think, "I will do **BETTER** than my best". You are back to the conclusion of the last paragraph. You negotiate to win. Nothing more: nothing less. In truth, that is your best.

A useful observation - you are not a dreamer, you are a doer.

You have entered the negotiating chamber knowing what you desire and the price that you prepared to pay. That desire may be a new house, a new car, goods for your business and so on. Furthermore, you know that you are going to succeed. Picture yourself and your family sitting in that new house, driving a brand new car home or profitably selling those goods in your business at a nice profit...Picture in your mind your desire and you are well on the way to achieving it. That really is true confidence building.

2 KNOWING, AS FAR AS IS POSSIBLE, WHAT THE COMPETITOR WANTS

A delightful tree is only a delightful tree because it has a fine root system that supplies most of its needs to keep it alive and well. Likewise a successful negotiation is only money making because of all the work and thought that has been undertaken before the competitors meet. Back to the trees - take away the root system and the tree will wither and die. If you do not undertake any work and/or deliberations before you take part in a negotiation and...well, that's it, you will suffer and probably lose the negotiations. A useful quote from Hamlet - "Nothing comes out of nothing".

A major part of the "root system of dealing" is knowing what the competitor wants. A useful suggestion - it is beneficial to realise that you cannot hit a target without knowing that the target exists. How can you successfully negotiate unless you have an idea of what you are aiming at and, as vital, have a good (general) idea what the competitor is aiming to achieve.

Before gaining a true idea of what a competitor desires it is useful to take a stab at assessing his character. You will really be taking a stab for, unless he is known to you or is well-known in the district, it is impossible to other than make an intelligent guess. When you first meet an unknown competitor there is only a minute or two to form a general opinion. Quickly you must try to ascertain what makes him tick. Is he a stubborn person? If so, do not rush him. Is he too eager to do a quick deal? Then, if the terms suit you - do it. Do not plod along until he gets bored and turns away. Do you detect that money is his main concern? Then, start talking money and show what a great bargain he is being offered. You will learn to judge from his first words, from his body movements, from his general demure, from the way that he endeavours to get the negotiations moving, et al.

You see, firstly, you seek to ascertain his character. A general guide will be helpful when the serious business begins. Secondly, you endeavour to ascertain his real desire. Now, that is not easy. You may get a clue from his approach. You are more likely to be able to get a glimpse of his desire as the haggling progress. For example, if the negotiations are dragging be direct and ask, "I`ve increased my offer twice to £3,600. You have not reduced your price at all. May I ask you, please, if it is worth me negotiating any further? Are you saying that £4,250 is not negotiable? Come on. Don`t let us waste time". He is compelled to answer those two questions. You should learn much from his answer - or lack of an answer. Remember, your ultimate goal is your own target - do not get bogged down in his character or his desire to the detriment of your own case. If you cannot ferret out this information, do not waste time. Move on and push towards your own objective.

At the commencement of a negotiation one of the parties is likely to have an advantage.

IF YOU HAVE THE ADVANTAGE. You have no need to give any ground. Talk and politely illustrate your advantage. You are on the way to winning the battle. Make the competitor realise that he has no chance in Hell of coming out of the confrontation on the winning side. But, beware. The odds on favourite can and does lose. If you feel that your advantage is slipping away immediately reinforce your position. Keep plugging your advantage so that it is not forgotten. Use motivation, which is dealt with in the next Essential. Explain in a clear and vivid way your advantage. Emphasise that it is not only to your benefit. It is to his gain to seize the exceptional proposition that you are putting forward. **Clearly** explain that you have the advantage but, even so, the goods or services that you are offering are first-class and he would be unwise not to deal. A useful reminder - never forget that it is possible to lose even the best advantage if you are in any way lax or too confident.

IF YOUR COMPETITOR HAS THE ADVANTAGE. You must still endeavour to seize the initiative. This can be done by way of questions. Why does he consider that your goods are not first-class, as you know them to be? You should work in - where has he seen better goods? Then, with tongue in cheek, why didn`t he buy them? Those goods that can be purchased cheaper that yours - are they the same good quality? Of course not, you have seen cheaper goods - but the quality!! Do not let him get away with vague accusations; make him give you real facts and figures. Questions will drain away his confidence and advantage. He may still have that advantage but you have blunted its value by grabbing the initiative.

The above examples assume that you are the seller. You have seen how profitable it can be to turn an argument your way. However, you could be a buyer. As an exercise, stop reading and commit to paper the actions that you would take if you knew that a seller was desperate to sell. It could be that you are aware of his cash flow problems or that he is overstocked. Discreetly exploit those (your) plus points. The seller may only want to sell if the price is over market value. He is known to be a very wealthy trader whose lifestyle does not depend on a profitable trading scenario. Now, that is a challenge. Think about ways to tackle that difficult job.

This Essential ends with a useful suggestion and applies if the business is really wanted or is substantial and it would be worthwhile to do a little detective work before meeting your competitor. Find out his character, his reliability, his present day commitments...there is bound to be a local business person known to you who knows him. It would be of great help to know what he is buying and/or selling. Is he involved in any large undertaking that may give a hint that he wants urgently cash/and or materials? You may have the very asset that he needs. With some gained information you can happily go into the negotiating chamber.

3 BUILD YOUR CASE TO REFLECT (1) AND (2)

This essential includes indispensable guidance which will be beneficial as you face the competitor; that is, when you are in action.

Salesmanship is every bit of discussing, listening, exchanging of views and debating (not arguing) points of which there is disagreement and, hopefully, arriving at a satisfactory and reasonable conclusion. Do remember that listening is essential.

A word of warning - on no account be afraid of competition. Do not get cold feet before you start. Competition is the life blood of nearly everything - business, sport, entertainment, et al. Without it salespersons/negotiators would not be required. You would be unemployed. No bargaining; no negotiating - it is as simple as that. Therefore, be proud of you job and of your career. You are an essential clog in the wide world of business. Go into your haggling with those positive thoughts in mind. At the back of your mind is another driving force - fail on too many occasions and you will be amongst the jobless. That will truly unsettle you and goad you into doing more that your best on all occasions.

Whether you know the competitor or not it is courteous to start a meeting on a pleasant tone. A few pleasantries will set the right tone. Ask about his holiday, his family, his job, his golf...but do not overdo it. You will both be eager to get down to work.

If you want something from someone be interested in that person and it will help you to attain your desired goal. That is a cynical observation, yet there is a lot of truth in it. Such interest is created by politicians at every general election. It is you - the elector - who matters...until the votes are counted! That superficial interest in persons is not the aim that you seek. You must have a **genuine** interest in others. You display both interest and sincerity. Having said that, there are times when you must add a little acting to your sincerity.

The majority of buying and selling is transacted face-to-face. However, despite that there is always someone else involved although not present. There are other persons out there in the wide world who would love to have the opportunity to buy or sell the commodities you are discussing. That is the unseen competition that exists. It has a considerable bearing on every aspect of salesmanship. Without those unseen persons negotiating would be so much easier.

THE SELLER AND THE UNSEEN COMPETITION. The possible buyer is, in effect, saying that if the seller will not sell at his (the buyer's) price there are others who have similar goods and will (may?) do so. So, that is a constraint on the seller. The possible buyer balks. He believes that he can do better elsewhere. He walks away and seeks that alternative seller. But, is he wise to do so?

THE BUYER AND THE UNSEEN COMPETITION. The seller is, in effect, saying that if the possible buyer will not buy at his (the seller`s) lowest price there are others who will (may?) do so. So, that is a constraint on the buyer. He can only get the seller down to a specific price, at that price the seller believes that he can do better elsewhere. He walks away and seeks that alternative buyer. But, is he wise to do so?

You will have noticed that the buyer and seller in the last two paragraphs both **assume** that there is an alternative source that is willing to do business on better terms. Neither can be sure. The operative word is "may" not "will". That is why when a party decides to walk away he must make a judgement as to whether or not he can do better elsewhere. Only experience and the knowledge of the market will help in coming to that decision. However, it is always a calculated risk. Also, to find that other source of business may be costly in terms of money and time. So often a bird in the hand...as is so often said.

It must be remembered that the law of supply and demand means that conditions are changing all the time. Markets rarely stand still. Hence, your tactics will have to adapt to the present day conditions. That is another compelling reason why you must know the market conditions inside out. If you are out-of date...well, you are on to a (near) certain loser. A perfect comparison is that you will be like a golfer trying to sink a thirty foot putt - blindfolded!

Yet another person who is both seen and heard lurks in the negotiating chamber. That person is a friend of the competitor; he can be dangerous and annoying. Often, to be a little heartless to him, he can be a real pest. That third person will almost always endeavour to show that he is a very clever individual. He must not be ignored. Tackle him head on. Do not ignore his comments. If he is correct - agree. If he is wrong - politely explain why. If he is such a pest that he is getting in the way of the negotiations you may be compelled to cease negotiating and arrange to talk to the competitor alone. That could upset the competitor. It will upset the third person. But, needs must be.

The problem is at its most aggravating when the third person has little or no knowledge of the subject being discussed. That is the real pest. However, you must pay attention to a professional or a person well-versed on the subject. Such a person is likely to help rather than hinder.

Are you talking to the right person? That is, a person who is able to conclude a deal without any ifs or buts. Not someone who will say, "We agree. I now have to obtain my boss`s approval". Often it is not possible to get an appointment to see the boss or a person who is able to give a firm decision without any conditions. If you do get, "I agree...but..." scenario you must try to get the provisional agreement firmed up to a definite decision as soon as possible. Consider this approach, "You and I agree. That`s fine, but I must have a firm decision by twelve noon on Friday - the 30th of August. Sorry to push you but my boss won`t take any action until we have a firm deal". Is it prudent to give that style of ultimatum? Certainly, it is a way to try to obtain a definite decision. But beware, you might get a revised offer or the competitor`s boss may walk away. That sad state of affairs may not have been brought about by your ultimatum; he was probably going to walk away in any event. A boss can be a cunning and devious person who alters an agreed deal to his advantage. You see, an agreement subject to conditions is not a deal at all. It is merely a stage in the negotiations. Have the courage of your convictions and put the competitor on the spot. Alternatively, you might deem it an artful move to ask to see immediately the boss or someone who can approve the deal. That could be embarrassing as it could upset the person who has agreed the conditional deal. So, take all circumstances into account before adopting that course.

Bernard Shaw said that money is the most important commodity in the world. The salesperson knows this to be true; he is talking and thinking money every minute of the working day. He generally talks of price and, of course, that means money. It is useful to know how price is used when dealing.

It is said that only a fool thinks that price and value are the same thing. Price is the amount of money that a seller asks for goods or services. In theory, a trader may ask what he likes for goods. In that respect, there is a free market. However and here is the rub, unless the price is fair value compared with similar goods on the market the chance of selling will be poor. That raises the next question. What is value? Value is the price that reflects the availability and cost of similar goods on the market. If there is a glut, value (obtainable prices) will fall. If a dearth, value (obtainable prices) will rise. Another factor that has a bearing on price is cost of producing the goods - but, that is a complex subject beyond the scope of this book.

A trader knows the market and will adjust prices to reflect the current market conditions. If he does not do so and prices fall, little if any business will be done. If prices rise and he does not increase prices, a useful profit will be lost and there will less cash available to replenish stock. It will be seen that a trader must really know and be able to read the market; otherwise his prices will not be in step with market conditions and he will lose out. The market, per se, must not be ignored. A certain lady said that you cannot beat the market. It is there, it rules price structure and, therefore, a negotiator must have some knowledge of market mechanism.

Another factor that governs value is the condition of the goods being offered for sale. A trader's price will only be correct if his goods are priced to truly reflect their condition. A negotiator is able to talk prices up and down depending on their condition as compared with similar goods on the market. For example, in a vegetable market a trader will get a higher price than other traders if his goods are of good quality - fresh and local produce will attract customers. Conversely, a trader at the next stall will get lower prices if his goods are of poor quality - foreign and looking tired. Prices do constantly change depending on both the availability and the condition of competing goods...and that is the meat of the salesman's patter.

As you negotiate you will get to know all the tricks of your trade and will be able to alter your patter to suit differing blends of price, value, condition and availability. There you have the fundamental principles of salesmanship. It operates through the haggling (movements) of the market.

One last observation on price/value. Never call your goods a bargain, a gift or a steal. That is a tired and unimaginative way of marketing. It is acceptable when used in a fairground; there it is part of the fun. Nevertheless, it is not sensible commercial salesmanship.

It is essential to go into the negotiating chamber with all the facts and figures at your fingertips. Imagine the scene. You are sitting facing the competitor. You worry, "Am I well-informed? Are my facts right? Consider the next three paragraphs.

Some time ago I was negotiating the sale of a dairy farm. It was a one off deal as I knew nothing about farming. I had a vague idea that there was such a thing as a milk quota. I telephoned a farmer friend and he kindly briefed me on milk quotas, dairy farming.et al. At the meeting with the owner/farmer I was able to throw in the question on the farm's milk quota and asked his plans relating thereto. The farmer asked my advice! The valuation of milk quotas is a very specialist exercise and I recommended an expert. After the meeting a colleague said he was greatly impressed with my knowledge of dairy farming and milk quotas. The lesson of this example is that without some research I would have been completely lost. A little research enabled me to appear reasonably capable - and I gained a sale.

Here are two interesting observations on appearing to be well-informed. Firstly, a book reviewer said that to have a passable knowledge of a newly published book you did not have to read the book - just read the review. Secondly, at a meeting a friend of mine gave a complicated and very hard-to-follow mathematical example relative to the subject being discussed. He asked if there were any questions. I doubt if any person present fully understood his reasoning. One person asked a rather vague question. After the meeting I told the questioner that I was very impressed with his knowledge. He smiled, "Didn't asking that question give me good publicity?" he patted me on the back and walked away. They say that any publicity is good publicity. I was not sure about that until I witnessed that questioner putting it into practice.

H G Wells said, "A little knowledge is a dangerous thing". Beware how you use that little bit of information that you gleaned from a reference book. Do not make it a leading part of your reasoning. Just pop it into a conversation as an aside. You are unlikely to be taken up on a vague remark which is concealed in a more substantive assertion. A useful reminder - if you possess only limited knowledge on a subject have your say and quickly move on.

However well prepared you are for meetings sooner or later there will come a time when a question is asked and you have no answer. When that arises be honest and clearly say that you do not have the answer. There are two alternatives. Firstly, offer to ascertain the answer and pass it on to the questioner. That will put the question to bed and the meeting can continue. Secondly, if it is a question that is absolutely vital to the negotiations it may be necessary to adjoin until the question can be resolved. Both of those ways of dealing with an unanswerable question is better that waffling on, losing the ear of those present and, hence, losing face...and, maybe, a deal.

The most soul destroying statement a competitor can make is, "You are wrong. That is just not right and I have proof that you are totally wrong". Bang! - You feel like a small boy being corrected by his school teacher. More so, you have lost many plus points and your chance of a successful deal is falling fast. Do not despair for ways in which a mistake or weakness should be tackled follow the following suggestions.

The very best salesperson, one at the top of his profession, will not go through business life without having to face some troublesome days. That is real everyday life, it throws problems at you when they are least expected. It is now necessary to consider what should be the response when there is a mistake or weakness on **your** side.

FIRSTLY, A WEAKNESS - There is no alternative - expose it at once. Tell the truth about it. Do not waffle on - be clear and show that you are fully aware of the problem. Do not disguise it. Get it well off your chest before the competitor throws it in your face. As an example, it is known by nearly everyone in town that your firm is in trouble. That is a serious weakness. You are endeavouring to sell surplus stock. Here is a way to talk to a possible buyer. "You may have heard the **rumour** (Comment: accent on the word **rumour**) that my business is in trouble. Well, it isn`t as bad as that. I admit that times are hard. To be fair, I must tell you that this surplus stock is only for sale at realistic prices. Please do not think that I`m desperate and will sell at silly prices. I would rather keep the stock and sell when business improves than sell at silly low prices now". If put over in the right manner that statement will show a degree of confidence. If the competitor does not believe you and will not talk sensible prices you move on.

The last paragraph illustrates that a weakness must be disclosed and disposed of by covering it up in a display of confidence.

SECONDLY, A GENUINE MISTAKE - Again, there is no alternative. Immediately expose it. Apologise and then put the matter right by giving the correct version. A useful suggestion - there is no merit in trying to hide a mistake. Eventually it will rear its ugly head and the cost of the hidden mistake being exposed by a competitor is likely to be very high. The lesson is this - cut the cost and expose without any delay. Never admit openly that you have made a mistake. Talk round it. For example, call it a slight error that needs putting right as you do not want to mislead. It may gain you some plus points if you make great play that you must get the matter absolutely clear as you have no wish to deceive anyone.

It is a different and happier event when the competitor has the burden of a weakness or mistake on his side.

FIRSTLY, HIS WEAKNESS - It is likely to be a disadvantage. He must sell, he needs money **now**, he is going to live abroad, his goods are perishable and must be sold today, et al. Ruthlessly expose and then exploit in a gentlemanly way. Keep saying that the money is here now. Can he afford to wait? Put your cheque book or cash on the table - let him smell the money that he urgently needs. Throw in that you are, of course, very sympathetic; that may soften the blow. If he will not deal do not walk away. Chat about another mutual subject. You are his only hope. He is desperate and may grab your lifeline and haul himself out of the mire

SECONDLY, HIS MISTAKE - Treat it in the same manner as a weakness although you can be tougher. Make it seem that he is purposely trying to mislead you. That will really put him off guard; no one likes to be caught cheating or being accused of cheating. OK, it was probably a genuine mistake; even so assumed accusation will unsettle him. Everything is fair in love, in war...and in negotiating. The haggling can continue by saying something along these lines, "Despite your regrettable mistake (Comment: That makes you sound like a good guy) I`ll still offer..."That rubs it in and at the same time implies that the offer would have been the same if no mistake had been made. Of course, that is not true but it is a useful display of fairness.

A salesperson/negotiator must look at the world as being full of opportunities. In order to reap a fair harvest that ideal must be kept in mind in all situations. You see, without any doubt, a really true salesman is an opportunist. During all negotiations there will be twists and turns which may well mean that your set plan has to be rejigged or set aside. That does not matter if you see a better chance of success. In those circumstances at no time be hidebound, always be flexible and bring into play your powers of improvisation. Always grab opportunities. A suggestion to remember - grab and use all beneficial opportunities quickly before they disappear. Do not only look and listen, you may miss the jackpot that you have been seeking. Take action.

Another word of warning is needed - Only grab that opportunity when it relates to the immediate negotiations. For example, if your bid for a mass of scrap iron is £25,000 and the owner lets it slip that it cost him £15,000, take him on immediately and find a good reason for reducing your bid. Ask for a further inspection and, lo and behold, you find that you have made a mistake. It is not the mix that you thought. Or, you find too much rusty material. "Sorry for that silly slip up. Nevertheless, I`ll bid £20,000". You may end up doing a deal between £20,000 and your "wrong" bid of £25,000. On the other hand, of course, your competitor may walk away.

Referring to the negotiations in the last paragraph; if the owner said as an aside that he had fifty wrecked cars for sale listen and put that information in your memory bank. To start talking about the wrecked cars will take both his and your thoughts away from the scrap iron. You went to the yard to buy the scrap iron. Clinch that deal and, if you want to buy fifty wrecked cars start talking about them **after** you have bought the scrap iron.

From the last paragraph you will realise that by complicating a deal and bringing in an unrelated matter it may result in you losing the deal that you desired. Some salespersons would try to negotiate for the scrap iron and the fifty wrecked cars as one overall deal. I would not do that; it may result in a more difficult deal to negotiate. A useful suggestion - tie up the deal that you set out to do. Then, come what may, your time has not been wasted. You are now on a friendly business footing with the owner, if you want the wrecked cars start talking...with a new found friend.

When trying to buy an item the price is generally the most important consideration. All prospective purchasers immediately ask, "How much?" When an advertisement states, "Offers invited". I know from experience that every caller is, in the first instance, not interested in the good; his first question is, "What is the price or guide price?" That is fair enough. But, all good salespersons know that everything is open to negotiation - not only price. As an example, a lounge suite is offered for sale with delivery in twelve weeks. That condition of delivery could be challenged. An interested person states, "OK, the price is about right (Comment: never admit that the price is right. It is always **about** right), but I must have delivery in four weeks. I move to a new house next week and have guests staying with me in three weeks. So, twelve weeks delivery is out of the question". The seller has a buyer if the suite can be delivered in four weeks. The seller must go back to his supplier and negotiate with him. Otherwise he has lost a buyer.

If the price is causing concern and negotiations look like breaking down it is often possible to bring life back into the haggling by considering conditions. As an example, when trying to buy a car but you cannot quite agree the price. The car has four well-worn tyres. Increase your offer to include four new tyres being fitted. A seller anxious for a deal may be tempted and may overlook the true cost of providing and have fitted four new tyres. A true negotiator may offer two new tyres...and so it goes on. Another example, the owner of a house will not accept your offer although it is very close to the asking price. You know that he is desperate to sell. Slightly increase your offer with completion in two week from that day. Cash in two weeks at a price very close to the asking price is an attraction to an owner anxious to sell.

A useful summary - in the final analysis price is always the prime consideration. Yet, other factors linked with price can usefully form part of the negotiations. As previously stated, everything is open to bargaining. As they say, there are more ways of killing a cat...but, remember that cash is always king. As previously stated it is a super ploy to put cash or your cheque book on the table. A person anxious to do a deal may be tempted by seeing the real McCoy.

It is imperative to dispose of all insignificant matters at the start of the negotiations. These are likely to be of minor concern but may well have a bearing on the haggling if left unanswered. As an example, you have inspected a bungalow and both your wife and you have fallen in love with it. Other than price there are two questions that you want answered. Firstly, when can the owner give possession? Secondly, is all the equipment in the fully fitted kitchen included in the quoted price? The estate agent's details are not clear on this point. If these questions are left unanswered they may get in the way of negotiations on price.

Another example, a second-hand car is being purchased and the price has been agreed. The seller, a slightly devious man, has made a great song and dance of the fact that there is a valid MOT. The buyer, being a little wet behind the ears, did not ask to see the MOT certificate. Just before writing the cheque to purchase the car and a little late in the day, he asked when the MOT certificate expired. He did not like the answer and he walked away. It expired in seven days. When offering the car the owner should have been honest and/or the interested viewer should have asked to see the MOT certificate. Then, a sale might have been agreed and much time saved. A typical case of not getting a vital important subsidiary matter out of the way before a deal is negotiated and agreed.

It is the salesperson's overriding task to find out why the competitor wants to buy or sell and working on that information lead him to the close. That sounds far too easy - take it from me that is not so. The prime task is to work on what you have ascertained as being his desire (target). You must motivate him towards his own desire. He is not truly motivated until you start negotiating. Unless you know or have an idea of his **real** desire, what have you to motivate? OK, it is realised that the competitor would not be sitting opposite you unless he was interested in the lorry that you have for sale. You probe - why he wants to buy a lorry and you work on that. Your prime task is to make sure that he buys **your** lorry. So, you have to convince him that **your** lorry is the ideal one for his need. As an example, you already know that the competitor has to start a job tomorrow. He has told you (Comment: a bad negotiator) that his only lorry caught fire yesterday morning and is a complete wreck. What an opportunity you have. Well, you tell him, here is a suitable lorry and it is available now. It is taxed for six months. Can you do better than that in the time available?

To get familiar with motivation look the word up in any dictionary. You will see that it is ambition, desire, drive, wish, incentive, motivating force...I like the last description. A motivating force that makes a person move. A force that a salesperson uses to persuade a competitor that he (the competitor) really needs for a specific purpose the goods on offer

An example, a newsagent wants to sell the business and retire to Spain. You have inspected the property and the books. You are getting on well with the owner until price is discussed. You have a professional valuation someway below the asking price. You know that the business has been on the market for over ten months and that the owner is frantic for a sale. His new villa in Estepona is standing empty and his retirement is on hold. When discussing price keep bringing in that you can complete a purchase as soon as it suits him with all cash and no loan. His retirement could commence without further delay. How you wish that you could live in Spain -with all that sunshine. Do not be that blunt...but talk around it. Keep softly, softly working on it. The motivation is his chance of starting a long delayed retirement without further hold-up. Additionally, your cash offer is well above the professional valuation. He is getting a good financial deal. It will be realised from this example that you are using the seller's known circumstances to motivate him. That is an ideal negotiating situation.

When a friend shows you an item that he has just acquired he says, "Look what I have just **bought**" - he may use the word "purchased". Rarely do you hear, "Look what I have just been **sold**". The reason that the words "bought" and "purchased" are used is that we all hate having an item sold to us. We like to be in complete control or, more realistically, like to think that we are in control. Therefore, when selling lay stress that the competitor is buying the item. In the mind of most buyers there is a vast difference. He is in complete control of the negotiations and thinks, "You can`t sell me anything; "I`ll buy what I like". It will pay if you remember that when applicable; use it during (suitable) haggling.

You are advertising a fine antique desk in the press. Times are hard, business is poor. It is the end of a depressing week. You return to your shop and find that, despite market conditions, there are nine callers who have `phoned about the desk. You telephone the first three on the list and, for some reason or another, each one says that it is not what they seek. You are depressed and go home. Now, that is really being defeated without finishing the job. This is the action that you should have taken. Firstly, pull out of the gloom and get down to business. Secondly, telephone the six other persons on the list. On the law of averages one of those six may be the buyer that you seek. By calling only the first three on the list how could you have been sure that one of the other six were not going to do business with you? Each one called you, so there must be some interest. Callers do not telephone in answer to an advertisement for fun. You must ring all nine. You may do business with the ninth one.

A useful tip - do not pick and choose. Only a one hundred per cent effort is likely to be rewarding. Cutting corners or eliminating someone or something is not the way to a successful sell. You may eliminate the best chance. A missed chance rarely comes your way again. Make sure that you do not miss it the first time round. As you have already read - make it a rule always to be persistent. Never pick and choose - pick **every** opportunity.

A popular saying reminds us that silence is golden and, when negotiating, beneficial. It may be good tactics to ignore a remark that you have no wish to answer. Treat it as though it had not been said. You did not hear it. If the competitor repeats the remark you will have to answer.

Often it is useful to remain silent. But, other times you want to speak and cannot stop the competitor speaking. How do you break into a competitor's tirade? One way is to let him go on until he is exhausted. That is not a sensible solution as it will look as if you are accepting all or most of what he is saying. It is a delicate situation caused by another person's bad manners.

You may think that it is a good ploy to break in and loudly and firmly proclaim that you agree such-and-such a statement. That is likely to be taken as a sign that he is winning you over; he may be confident enough to stop and let you talk. To stop him you may have to say that you agree when, in realty, you do not. Even so, you have the floor and can express your own views. However, you must forthwith correct the false impression that you are in agreement. For example say, "Sorry, but I believe that I misheard you. I thought that you said..." and quickly move on.

If the competitor is a real tyrant and talks on as if you do not exist there is only one course to take. You must be blunt, be rude and demand to be heard. Be very frank. Occasionally that is the only way to get a fair hearing. Incidentally this is one of the few occasions when I advise being rude. Nevertheless, do not be too rude. Try to tinge your remarks with humour.

Picture the scene. The competitor that you face is a real charmer. He gives all the right answers. Gradually you are being charmed (talked) into a deal to buy goods on his terms. You find yourself agreeing that the goods are first-class and that the price is right. He is talking and acting in a manner which has deluded you. You have forgotten that old negotiating adage - never be talked into a deal. Suddenly you wake up and realise that you are not using all the experience that you possess. Before it is too late you snap back into action in an effort to save the day. That episode is a reminder that as good as you think you are you can still relapse into those old harmful ways. Always be on your guard as it will happen to you unless you are constantly wide awake and yearning to win every haggle. Let this paragraph be a warning to you.

In theory, you should give a little, take a lot. Well, life does not work like that. Often you have to take a little and give a lot. But, you try to do that on your terms when you know that it is in your interest to do so. You give more than expected and know, despite the (assumed) benefit that the competitor is being given, you are getting nearer your desired result. In reality, you are not giving away an advantage; you are giving away a little something in one hand and receiving a benefit that takes you nearer your target in the other. You are prepared to lose the skirmish so as to win the war. A useful suggestion - you must not give unless it is absolutely necessary to advance your case. Always have your desired result in the foremost of your thoughts. Every action and every word must have that end result in mind.

Negotiating is making concessions and still leaving some more room, if necessary, for further concessions. If you do not leave some room for further negotiations you may have made your final move - you may look weak and beaten.

When negotiating it is imperative to keep to the purpose. Do not waffle. Do not keep talking to show that you are clever. Put your argument in as short and simple manner as is necessary to present it clearly. Put and keep plus points to the fore; bad points, if it is necessary to discuss them, are put towards the end of your reasoning. Always end on a note that is likely to worry and/or depress the competitor. Answer questions promptly, clearly and as briefly as possible. Do not take that advice to mean that the answer must be brief for the sake of being brief. It must be both brief and understandable. If a question can only be answered in a longish answer, then act accordingly. It is better to be somewhat verbose and get the message across than concise and misunderstood. In other words, always be brief as is consistent with giving the right information in the correct manner.

Consider the reverse of the situation in the last paragraph. A waffling competitor is trying to confuse you. Be ruthless. Tell him in no uncertain terms that you are lost. Could he, please, put forward his argument in a more understandable manner? That will help to undermine his confidence. Do not put up with a waffling and wandering competitor. But, he may spill a few beans and you may well hear something to help you. Listen and do not protest until you are sure that he has no more to disclose. Do not forget that he who waffles - discloses.

It is essential that a salesperson does not get into a position where there is no escape. That will mean loss of faith. In the main, this means not committing yourself to a proposition without having considered fully its consequences, particularly its downside. Be careful what you say and do not be pushed into saying words which, even as you utter them, you realise should not be said. There is no escape from that carelessness. It is so easy to get committed by merely nodding or weakly agreeing. Again, there is no escape. You will only be able to remedy the position by looking as though you are going back on your word. That will harm your case. A useful suggestion - be very careful so that the competitor's trap does not snap shut with you in it. Constantly be wary. As your powers of salesmanship improve all this will become second nature to you. I have a rule - always keep the escape hatch open. If you gamble have a back-up in case it fails. Not easy, but well worth considering before you throw the dice.

Beware, do not expect that a competitor will easily release you from a trap. It will be tightened so that he gets as much benefit as possible. He will be laughing all the way to the close. Everyone wants their pound of flesh. That illustrates that you must do your best to keep away from traps and cul-de-sacs.

One of my favourite songs taught me many lessons. The song says, "You have to accentuate the positive, eliminate the negative..." The message could not be clearer. Be positive, be decisive, be constructive...from this sentence it will be realised what being positive is all about. The song goes a little further and we hear that the negative must be eliminated. Absolutely correct. A negative salesperson will find it much harder to sell or buy. In fact, it is almost impossible to convince a competitor when the salesperson himself is not convinced.

Often you have to say, "No thanks". When selling it is comparatively easy to turn the negative into a positive. As an example, a prospective buyer makes a silly low offer. You want to say, "No thanks" in rather a hostile way. To reply in a negative - even a polite one - is just not good enough. You are an experienced salesperson so consider saying, "Thanks for your offer. I consider that my price is realistic and gives good value. Think about it before we part. You are unlikely to do better elsewhere". Not a negative in sight. You have pleasantly brushed aside a silly offer and tried for a more realistic one. You have (you hope) collected the competitor's thoughts. The lesson is that you must learn to reply in the negative in a positive tone. Being a receptive person you would have noticed that the offer was not only politely refused; there was an attempt to keep the haggling going by inviting the competitor to think again.

Do you find yourself saying "yes" when you know in your heart of hearts that you ought to be saying "no"? You must learn to say "no" affably and refuse to say "yes" when the answer must be "no". Some persons are, in certain circumstances, shy of saying "no" and that gets them into an awful lot of trouble. You must shake off that inhibition. On the other hand, some persons hate being rejected. A thoughtless and curt "no" may upset the boss, a colleague, a good friend, the mother-in-law, et al. When it is necessary to say "no" always explain why and do it in a considerate way. An example, often it is difficult and embarrassing to reply to a request in the negative. You answer in the affirmative without thinking or because you do not have the nerve to say, "No thank you".

Consider this example, it is early in the morning and you are extremely busy. Your golfing friend telephones and invites you to make-up a foursome that afternoon. You do not want to let him down; if you do the three players will have to play an uninteresting three ball match. Whilst you are thinking of an excuse you find yourself arranging the time to meet at the club house. You are losing more time as you accept his offer to lunch. You put the 'phone down and wonder when the jobs which have to be completed by tomorrow afternoon will be finished. The lesson from this episode is simple and of benefit to all salespersons. Do not be tempted to say "yes" when you know that you must say "no". In this example, the three or so pleasant hours spent on the golf course should have been spent in the office completing those urgent jobs. There is no doubt that you should have said "No thanks, I'm so busy. I would love to but..." That is tough, isn't it? Real life is just like that - tough and unyielding.

One of the attributes of a top flight salesperson/negotiator is being able to walk away from what is turning out to be a bad deal. He will not be talked into a deal against his better judgement, will not be hassled, will be his own master and will only close a deal when he has truly what he set out to achieve. No ifs; no buts. A useful suggestion - it is easy to walk away, depressing to look back in anger on a poor deal. Never be troubled by an annoying thought, "If only I had walked away".

Never boast of your past successes, your wealth or your (assumed) fame. That is pure swank. It will not show confidence, quite the reverse. It tries to hide lack of confidence and puts in its place a false brave front. In any event, where will it get you? It gets you disliked. Therefore, if it is your wish to be successful, to be wealthy, to be famous, et al...that is fine. Live all those life styles and keep quiet.

Conversely, can it be beneficial to talk oneself down? On rare occasions it may be acceptable, even profitable. As an example, "You know more about that than I do (Comment: of course, not true), so will you explain it to me, please?" With that question you are trying to extract a useful something from a competitor. The question will make you look weak when you are strong. The competitor will be deceived and, thus, on the wrong foot. It is hoped that his explanation to you will trap him. It is a good ploy when you are fully informed on the subject and you know that the competitor is not. It could expose or cause a weakness or a mistake that you can ruthlessly exploit.

You have done your very best and are getting nowhere. Instead of walking away try this gambit. Manoeuvre the competitor into a position where your proposal is either accepted or he walks away. Embarrass him. Put the ball firmly in his court. Put your very best offer before him and say, "I`m sorry to say that we are getting nowhere. Time is so very valuable to us both; in an effort to come to terms, so as not to waste the time already spent this morning, I`ll sell on these special terms..." Those terms will be the lowest you are willing to accept. If not accepted you will have no qualms. You did more than your best. You stood your ground and showed that on realistic terms you wanted to do business. You did not walk away -he did.

4 CLOSE THE DEAL
BEFORE IT GOES AWAY

The close is the last step in the negotiating process. It is win, draw or lose time. It is dealt with in the next chapter. It is briefly mentioned here as all the hard work mentioned in (1), (2) and (3) must be brought to a conclusion. The conclusion is the close. Read on.

4
REAL SITUATIONS

This chapter is entitled Real Situations as you will be coming across some actual conditions met every working day. You will find that certain situations are discussed in other parts of this book. As previously explained that is because they are of such import that it is not possible to mention a specific aspect of negotiating without their involvement. To only include those items in this chapter would detract from their eminence. In truth, you are lucky for this is another opportunity of getting to grips with some of the indispensable aspects of your trade.

It cannot be stressed too often that it is the first move that always start the action. You are no doubt thinking that that is an obvious observation. Generally, I agree. However, when engaged in negotiations it is not as obvious as you think. Consider the example in the next paragraph.

As a property developer I had to find sites for redevelopment. If I waited in my office for estate agents to call with likely propositions I would have been bored. More to the point, my company would have gone bust. I went out looking for sites and drove around urban areas seeking properties with large gardens or where two or so properties could together form a developable site. All those doors that I knocked on were opened by owners who had no idea that their homes and/or gardens could be part of a housing development. You see, I put sites together by getting up, going out and creating business. The owners involved and my company would not have been benefited unless I had started the ball rolling. I am not boasting for it was comparatively easy work. It does dramatically illustrate that it is always the first move that matters. To put it another way, someone must start every activity.

My experience mentioned in the last paragraph does prove that my personal motto must be obeyed. It was during that period that the motto came to mind and I have had it before me ever since. A reminder - **NOTHING HAPPENS UNLESS YOU MAKE IT**...boring but true! The accent is, of course, on the **YOU**. So, you do not think that it will help you? Do not take my word for it. Try it. I know that it will be of great benefit to you...maybe, it will become your personal motto. Consider this second motto, which I thought about when it was a toss-up between working and playing a round of golf - nothing comes without work. Sad, but true!

To summarise, to act or not to act - that is not a question; it is a necessity...one must act. A useful reminder - act and win; do not act and you will never win. I remember reading an advertisement in a Sunday newspaper "What happens when you don`t advertise? The answer is loud and clear - nothing!" a first-class advertisement for advertising. Again the message is clear - do not act and you do not prosper.

Any business meeting or personal get-together can easily become dull, colourless and/or depressing. Sometimes all three words describe one meeting. That state of affairs can harm negotiations. If only there was a simple way to improve such meetings, to bring smiles to the faces of those gloomily gathered round the table. Sadly there is no instant cure. There is, however, a way of helping to obtain a degree of improvement which often does the trick. It is this - introduce just a little humour/wit into the proceedings. I have often done this and it really does help. Here is a word of warning which must be respected when using this course of action.

Never in any event make a joke or introduce any wit which can be construed as referring to any person at the meeting. No one will like to be the butt of your humour and will seek revenge. The joke/wit must be of a general nature and never about religion, race or politics. Keep all three well away from the negotiating table. Conversely, make yourself the butt of a weak and inoffensive joke. That is likely to get a competitor smiling. He may not notice the sting in it that helps your side of the haggle.

I have often brought a touch of humour into negotiations which have hit a rocky patch. That does not mean that all is saved. It does mean that the parties can depart from the scene with smiles on their faces and on good terms. That is so much better than departing on bad terms. Remember, it is a small world and you may meet again.

The next section deals with that annoying individual the person whose mind is closed, completely closed to reason and will not listen to any ideas or suggestions whatsoever. A person whose only interest is in himself and his own affairs. You do not exist. There are several reasons why a person displays those characteristics. It might be by following in father's footsteps and unable to deviate therefrom, by a genuine although misguided idea that all good negotiators act in that fashion, by a feeling that if he gives a little he may be forced to give a lot...Whatever the reason the problem is that the closed mind must be opened or, at the very least, probed so that a useful nugget or two are revealed.

When facing a closed mind it is helpful to remember that there is always during all negotiations a conflict between legitimate interests. It follows that at the start of negotiations a general exchange of views should take place between the opposing parties. To get such an exercise started is not a difficult exercise. But when one of the parties is a closed mind it is the most annoying and burdensome operation. The other competitors are talking to themselves. Still, needs must be, and an effort must be made to hold a general review even with a closed mind present.

Over the years I have seen many closed minds lose good deals and express regret immediately thereafter. One such incident stays in my mind. I recall the family of the majority owner of a family business pleading with him to accept an offer for the business. The offer was well over market value as the freehold had a special price to the prospective buyer. The owner's mind remained closed - until it was too late. Subsequently he said to me that "he had let the deal of the century get away". I remember five words that he repeated several time - "I'll never get over it". I mention this sad episode for two reasons. Firstly, when dealing with such a person keep trying. Then try, try and try again. If there is to him a special benefit in the proposition keep repeating it until it sinks in - or you believe it has sunk in. Much time has to be spent with such a person. Do not regard such time as wasted. Of course, there will be many occasions when you are getting nowhere. Then, as time is so valuable it must not be thrown away, pack up your papers and move on. Secondly, never get on the wrong side of the fence and become a close mind person, even for just one negotiation. Fight hard and be reluctant to give even a small concession. That is true negotiating. To close your mind when a proposition is put to you may mean that you miss a good deal. A closed mind person will seldom thoroughly examine a proposal and, hence, may lose out by being badly briefed and pig - headed.

To try to open a closed mind is like trying to open a locked door without the key. It is a near impossible task unless the door is broken down. Verbal force will rarely open a closed mind. It is more than likely to close it further. The closed mind person will be against everything that you say. The louder you (figuratively) shout, the tighter his mind will close. He will not budge. He knows (thinks) that he is correct. He reasons without a shadow of doubt that you are in the wrong. Why should he move an inch and agree with you. Here are some ways which may help to open a closed mind.

FIRSTLY, listen very carefully to what is being said. Do this so that it seems that you are really interested in his views. When he makes a remark with which you agree clearly express your agreement. The competitor will take it as a sign that he is winning. You only agree if that agreement will help you. Nevertheless, if he thinks that he is winning he may relax a little and make a disclosure that will help you. Keep up the pretence that he is getting the better of you. Say, as an example, "You're more au fait with that than I am" or "You know I never realised that before...tell me some more about it..." Do not let the chat slip so that he thinks that you are winning. That will surely result in the mind being more tightly closed. He will quickly higher the drawbridge.

SECONDLY, seek an area of positive agreement and put it before him in a friendly business manner. Do not be too friendly; a close mind considers that being friendly is dangerous and will involve giving away important data. If, as stated in the last paragraph, words have been said with which you agree that is fine. You have an area to explore together and for you to exploit. At that time help him to feel that he is winning, although doubts are being surreptitiously placed in his mind. You are endeavouring to penetrate his armour. Never in desperation agree just for the sake of agreeing. At all costs avoid being caught in a trap set by yourself. Never get hoist by your own petard.

THIRDLY, all of us love to be right and admire the person who reinforces our own (self) opinion. That is why you never use the word "wrong ". When you say, "You are wrong..." those three words raise the hackles and the competitor will hate you and instantly seek revenge. When you are tempted to say that someone is wrong draw back, take a deep breath and use words like, "Is that so, please tell me some more?" and expressions of a similar meaning.

Rarely is a person one hundred per cent right. In fact, when talking to a closed mind you must always avoid saying or implying that you are right. To do so will make the task of opening his mind even harder. It is a good ploy to hint that he might be right - although you know he is wrong. For example say, "I`m very interested in the suggestion that your pottery is unique (Comment - you know that few pieces of pottery are unique but it is a good opening remark). Will you, please, elaborate on that?" He is likely to prattle on and try hard to convince you. Ask further questions. You are not saying that he is wrong, merely asking for additional evidence. The discussion is likely to arrive at a stage where the competitor has to admit in a half-hearted way that, "Maybe I haven`t got that quite right". The closed mind is now not so closed. Never relax when trying to prise open that closed mind. It is repeated - keep asking questions some of which should hint that he could be right. Do keep in mind that suggestion is often more persuasive than a firm direct statement. It lets the listener work it out himself.

FOURTHLY, a closed mind is unlikely to be opened by logic. It will sense that you are trying to reason acceptance on your side of the argument. He hates reason and throws a negative at each idea that you put forward. Logic is completely out. Only guile and keeping the competitor`s thoughts on the notion that he is right are likely to succeed. The word "guile" is used in the sense that you will be endeavouring to prise open the closed mind without your line of attack being obvious. That is crucial as a closed mind is on constant guard, always ready to defend its views. It will instantly sense any verbal or visible attack. Remember, it is closed not dim-witted. You must negotiate by being cunning and artful. It must be softly, softly; friendly, friendly and it must not be realised by the competitor that you are gradually opening his mind.

It is a good idea to endeavour to reach a point where you are looking at the problem together. You may be able to do so by saying, "I fully understand your position and have no problem with it. Let me explain mine..." or "Let us look at this together..." or similar words that offers a mutual attempt for a general discussion.

If all fails show faith in the competitor. A display of, "Of course, I am sure that you are a fair minded person and will listen to my assertions..." Butter him up in a sensitive low-key routine. See him - that is talk to him - as he likes to be seen. Say that you do really appreciate his views; does he appreciate and understand yours? Get him talking about both sides of the negotiations. You may get a glimpse inside that closed mind and get an idea of what he really wants. Gradually move the conversation so that he is talking about your proposition; point out the benefits to him...the more you get him talking the nearer you will be to a deal.

The above four suggestions can be used when generally negotiating and not only when trying to open a closed mind.

We now come to that fake negotiating tactic of splitting-the-difference. Only the poorest negotiator treats this device as a normal gambit. Although it has just been described as a fake negotiating tactic it can, in limited circumstances, be a useful and profitable weapon. Only when it is used indiscriminately is it a misused tactic. I know negotiators whose sole purpose seems to be to split-the-difference. Their tactics are very well-known to their competitors and are easily dealt with as shown below.

It is extremely easy to detect a spit-the-difference ploy. The competitor`s terms start very high when selling and very low when buying. He thinks that a trap has been set and hopes that a quick offer to meet half-way will entice you to close and he will reap the profit from his conveniently priced open shot. When facing that dilemma be frank. Explain that his terms are quite unreasonable and that yours, in your opinion, are today`s fair prices. To accept his proposal would not be a fair and square deal. Of course, it would suit him as he would profit by his most unrealistic (unreal) opening bid to obtain a bargain deal. The gap between you is too wide to bridge and there is no way that you could consider his suggestion to spit-the-difference.

If a competitor insists on his split-the-difference offer and will not budge you must be brutal. Rub in that time is being wasted and neither of you can really afford that luxury. Therefore, thanks for the offer and a polite goodbye. You linger - will he come back with a more sensible/realistic proposition? Or, if you think that it might break the impasse surprise him with a counter proposal as illustrated in the next paragraph.

You could be cunning and try to beat him with his own trick. He wants £20,000 for his car. You consider that it is grossly overpriced and worth a top figure of £15,000. You, being an optimist, offer £12,000. The owner comes straight back with a split-the-difference offer of £16,000. Obviously he has accepted that his price of £20,000 was too high. However you consider that £16,000 is still above its true value. The owner will not budge and keeps on saying that his split-the-difference offer is fair. Your wife is very keen on the car; you had better buy it! You explain that his proposal does not help as it leaves the suggested price above the car's true value. He does not argue about value; evidently he (silently) agrees with you. You say, "Look, I would like to do a deal with you but the car's value is below your price of £16,000". You give, if possible, the asking prices of two similar cars you inspected in the last day or so. You call attention to minor points relating to his car - four new tyres will soon be needed; that dent on the back bumper, are you sure that it has not been in a crash? Then, you make a proposal. "I'll split-the-difference between my offer of £12,000 and your price of £16,000. I'll give you £14,000 - cash on the spot, right now. That is my final offer". Note that you say, "...your price..." as that is now the selling price.

In mock auctions like that in the last paragraph who knows whether a deal was struck and, if so, at what price. The offer of £14,000 leaves you room to increase another £1,000 to £15,000 if needs be. That means that that you would be buying the car at what you consider to be its true market value. In real life, with the slings and arrows of outrageous, you rarely know what is going to happen next. That is why it is always wise to keep trying, to alter your tactics when considered desirable and, when appropriate, to use the oldest trick in the book - to try to split-the-difference. A useful suggestion - a good (wary) negotiator looks ahead of the present action and is as flexible as circumstances will permit. He is prepared to use even the most banal ruse to get and keep negotiations moving.

If it is obvious that a competitor will not budge from his split-the-difference proposal and it leaves the terms far from what you consider reasonable, you must be relentless. He has refused your counter split-the-difference suggestion and will not even discuss it. It is truly "thanks and goodbye" time. It is difficult to known when you have come to the end of the line. As illustrated above, it does no harm to linger to see if the competitor will have a last minute change of heart. Or, mention to him another subject that concerns you both. After that, who knows? All the time that you and the competitor are together there is hope. You will now realise that it is my policy to fight to the bitter end. That must be your policy, too.

Here are two further occasions when this device may be used:

FIRSTLY, you nearly have what you require from the haggling yet you cannot get the competitor to move that last little bit. You are so close. You have tried, tried and tried again - and have not yet been successful. There is only one action left. Offer to split-the-difference. As you nearly have what you require only a little will be given away. It is worth the effort to possibly gain that little extra. In those conditions you are using the device to close the deal. Do not forget it could result in a successful close or where you both walk away empty handed. Negotiations rarely go according to a preconceived plan and the completely unexpected does often suddenly happen. It that respect it is similar to most ploys, it must be used with prudence and there is never a one hundred per cent chance of being successful. You know that sometimes the salesperson/negotiator takes on the role of the actor. Additionally, he takes on the role of the gambler, although he will be bringing all his experience to each venture. Hence, the likelihood of success should be in his favour.

SECONDLY, there is no way that you can get the negotiations moving along. The competitor does not seem interested and you cannot follow his reasoning. Is he being standoffish to show that you face a tough negotiator? Does he consider that his goods are superior that the price should not be denigrated? Why doesn't he clearly state his views. Rather than call it a day desperate action is needed. Test him. Offer a split-the-difference proposal. It will soon be apparent if he genuinely wants to do business. A word of warning, you will be playing the wild card and may well upset him. He is not playing ball; he walks away. Well, at least, you have saved time and can seek some profitable business.

Let us consider a gloomy episode. The competitor keeps changing his mind. One minute it looks as if you might come to terms; the next, well, where are we going? All your attempts to be reasonable have failed. Well, not quite, for all salespersons know that there is (nearly) always another step that may bring a little brightness into the gloom. That next step is to give an ultimatum. That sounds like a desperate move which could well fail. In the place of gloom could be sheer darkness. The very end. That will not be the case if you only use an ultimatum in selected situations. An early warning, an ultimatum can so easily backfire. Equally, it can be an effective and a rewarding tactic to use.

An ultimatum is a way of saying to the competitor that here is a last chance. Accept it or else…now, that sounds fine but you cannot make him accept. You can threaten, bully, intimidate et al…and not get a response. Therein is the danger. What happens when you are left with an ultimatum that has been refused? What happens at a minute or two after twelve o`clock when the competitor did not take the bait at noon. That is why it is absolutely necessary to consider possible failure before striking out with an ultimatum. It is said that it does not matter what a man does if he is prepared to accept all the consequences of his actions. Recall that last sentence when you are about to give an ultimatum.

An ultimatum nearly always links time with price. To link those two indispensable and fundamental elements of salesmanship is asking for trouble. Bright red lights begin to flash. Here is an example of a simple and typical ultimatum -"We have spent so much time on this matter that I believe I am reasonable (Comment - You know you are not!) to give you one last chance. My final bid is £385,000 and I`ll give you until twelve noon tomorrow to accept. If you do not accept I will have no further interest in doing a deal on this property". Is that last sentence wise? The ultimatum itself is final, so why try to be extra tough? In any event, without that comment the owner may come back with an acceptable proposition. Never slam the door tightly shut.

Only on rare occasions have I used an ultimatum. When talks lead me to believe that failure is on the cards and we are many miles apart on price; it all seems hopeless. In those depressing conditions an ultimatum will tend to concentrate the competitor's thoughts. He will cogitate. He has to give an answer - to accept, to make another proposal or to walk away. At the very least, the ultimatum has made him act. Despite all the advice given you are acting the bully; but you are doing it diplomatically.

I know of one or two negotiators who are naturally extremely lucky. Each negotiates by using the ultimatum as if it will soon go out of fashion and rely, to a certain extent, on their knowledge and their luck. They know the risks involved. Their motto must be - nothing ventured; nothing gained. The average negotiator will not recklessly gamble as the lucky ones do and realises the implications when using the ultimatum. Even so, its use is always a gamble. So, before using it do weigh up all the pros and cons. Do not stick your neck out - unless you are one of those lucky persons who, remember, do not win on every throw of the dice.

Is it desirable to issue an ultimatum in an endeavour to close a deal? It can be very tempting. An ultimatum has an air of certainty. It seems to be implying that if it is not taken up that is the end of negotiations. In that respect it is, of course, a dangerous exercise. If what looked like a beneficial close is not accepted to the competitor a serious stalemate exists. In the right circumstances it might be less risky to force attempt a close by a split-the-difference offer. That is a less severe effort to force a close. It does not sound so final and does not push (bully) the competitor in the same way as an ultimatum. A useful suggestion - an ultimatum looks final; a split-the-difference exercise leaves the door wide open. Use the former if you want to end the haggling one way or the other; the latter if you want to test the competitor and leave room for haggling.

Conversely, you are faced with an ultimatum. It may be that the competitor has nothing else to offer, nothing more to say, he is desperate and knows it. You have completely outwitted him. That may be so, but you still have an ultimatum to answer. If it contains terms that are acceptable, accept and that is a deal done. If the terms are unacceptable it will be easy to upset him by making a counter ultimatum. Then, you will both be gamblers.

It might be a clever move to give a counter-ultimatum in the following manner. You are faced with a "...buy at £40,000 by noon tomorrow or I will sell elsewhere..." you are keen to buy and your last offer was a reluctant £37,500. You reply "...Thanks for your offer. I cannot go to £40,000. At that figure the goods are overvalued. Don't you agree? (Comment - silly question but it might get a reply). Let's have one last chance of doing a deal. I'll offer a top price of £38,500 if we do a deal NOW. Come on...it's up to you." The competitor is now on the spot. It is his decision time and he has nowhere else to go...although he could offer to split-the-difference again. That illustrates that there is always a fight back.

The next section of this chapter deals with the close of a deal. When running a five hundred metre race you are not sure that you have won until you pass the winning post. Likewise, with salesmanship you must not count your chickens until they are hatched - that is after a successful close. Only then has a deal been concluded. You may be within an ace of doing a deal, you relax and say a few wrong words or attempt to be too clever or greedy...and one of those wrong moves may turn what looked like being a good deal into just an ordinary every day one. The run-up to the close is an exciting yet dangerous time.

It will be known if "closing time" is approaching for within your grasp is the prize that you sought. It may not be the result that you desired at the start; you have given as well as received from the haggling. That does not matter as the conclusion is to your liking. Do not cry over spilt milk when there is enough in the jug. You are happy with the deal, so close.

Is the competitor ready to close? Does he see success on the horizon? Or, is he beginning to see that his terms are too harsh for you to accept? How you wish that you knew. Look and listen for signs that indicate a change in his thinking. Watch for words such as normally, generally, as a rule, usually, let us be reasonable, et al.

For example, he might say, "As a rule we don't reduce asking prices..." That is excellent. Is he about to break a rule and conclude a deal? Is he becoming a little more receptive to your reasoning? Listen for similar hints that he is weakening - and keep him moving that way.

A friend of mine said that he knew little about buying and selling and it seemed to him that negotiators were forever looking for advantages. That is both a splendid and wise observation. A simple comment and one that all salespersons must take to heart. It is relevant as the close approaches.

As seen both a split-the-difference attempt and an ultimatum may be a suitable way to endeavour to close. But, circumstances must be just right if their use is to be successful. Hold both in reserve. To you an ideal run-up to a close looks as though you are heading for a deal that is acceptable to both sides. That is really perfection and should be implied in all that you say. You may be excited because you are getting all or more that you sought. Great, but keep it to yourself. You do not want the competitor to sense that you are "over the moon" and to hike terms against you.

Sooner or later in some way or another you will have to indicate that a close is approaching. It has to be undertaken in a quiet no-nonsense way. This could be achieved by saying, "We have (Comment - that is a correct start as it confirms that both of you are involved in the close) nearly reached a scenario that suits us both..." or, "We are moving in the right direction and have nearly agreed..." There are many ways of expressing that sentiment. As previously stated, the objective is to keep before the competitor that you are concerned not only with your own interest, he and his business are as important. It is a mutual enterprise.

THE CLOSE - IF YOU ARE SELLING: It is essential that you close whilst there is still real competition. As an example, you are very lucky and you have three possible buyers. One has made a very attractive offer which will give you much more cash than expected. What do you do? You accept that offer and tell the other two that the item is sold. You see, you accepted a first-rate offer whilst there was real competition from the other two parties. If the two had been approached before a deal was concluded and they both withdrew, you go back to the person who made the excellent offer and...he hesitates. He senses from both your body movements and from what you say that he has no competition and lowers his offer below that "excellent offer". The prospective buyer with no real competition is king of the castle. Of course, you could start all over again by and money and may not guarantee another bid equal to the excellent one you lost. I repeat it is sound policy to close the deal whilst **there is still real competition.**

A useful suggestion - it is acceptable to upset one offerer by accepting a better offer from another bidder. It is disastrous to play one competitor against another and lose an excellent offer that you should have snapped up. The only sentiment when negotiating is to win. In the final analysis it is up to you - are you a somewhat cautious person or a gambler? If the latter you will realise from past experience that you win some and lose some and yet are still prepared to play one competitor against another to the bitter end. If a gambler you willing accept that the bitter end may, on occasions, be very bitter.

In the last but one paragraph reference is made to the "real competition" that exists when there is authentic competition and is not a figure of anyone's imagination. A word of warning - be wary if you decide to use that "figure of imagination" approach which is convincing you that a false competitor can be made to look real. An average competitor on his toes will easily sense that poor illusion.

With most sales situations there are other possible buyers and sellers out there in the world who might be willing to deal. They exist, are unseen and do not know of any specific negotiations taking place. Those possible competitors could be called "unseen competition". They are used by a salesperson by saying, "Of course, there are many persons out there who could well be interested in doing a deal with me..." The competitor's answer could be, "Of course there are. I couldn't argue otherwise. So, go out there and find them". A challenge not likely to be accepted.

To be absolutely clear, a buyer or a seller is always genuinely in touch with "real competition" whereas "unseen competition" is not in touch with, or knows of, the specific negotiations; yet it is there and could be converted into "real competition" through advertisements, contacts between salespersons, trade contacts and the like. Generally it cannot be converted into "real competition" in time to influence a specific and active negotiation.

So, when a negotiator tries to rely on this "unreal competition" he is thinking, also of all the "unseen competition" which he believes exists but which, at that specific point in time, is of little use to him. It is *nearly* a figure of his imagination.

THE CLOSE - IF YOU ARE BUYING: Entirely different circumstances exist. The endeavour is to knock out all other competition. If the competition is very active make an offer very close to your top figure. That may eliminate some of the other competitors and you will have a few pounds in hand. Push hard for a close. Make a vague suggestion that you are getting fed up. If at a meeting say, "I've another appointment later on this morning so time is running out. I'll increase to £51,000 and give you a cheque right now. I can't leave that offer on the table after...for long. (Comment - does that change in the last sentence hint at a possible ultimatum? It is said to be perceived as such)".

When all parties are not assembled at one place and only you and one competitor are present do your best and push hard for a close. If the seller will not close until he has spoken to the other parties tell him that you are seriously interested and will he come back to you before closing a deal with another party. If he agrees that is fine - but, you have more or less implied that you will increase your offer. When he comes back make your best offer after gleaning all you can about the other interests. If he will not agree to come back to you before selling make your highest offer and hope that it is not beaten by another bidder. When making that offer try to find out when he is seeing the other competitors so that you can call on him and ascertain what is happening. You are, of course, appearing too keen but needs must be.

You will now realise that when negotiating there is never a certainty, never a sure way in which a competitor is going to move. So, constantly be on the lookout for a competitor's change of mind or tactics. The twists and turns of haggling never cease to amaze me. Being at the scene of the action is like being in poll position in a Grande Prix and in a possible winning position...but still having to go all out to win!

Do not be that green-eyed monster unless you are a true gambler and prepared to accept all the risks. Consider this setting - you are about to close as the money that you required for your goods is on the table. You hesitate. You dream of a little more money. You think, "That's been too easy (Comment - it hasn't but you don't argue with yourself). A little more...just a few pounds more...that would be very nice. Of course it would..."...you again hesitate, "...but would the amount on the table remain?" The sensible thought should be, "I realise that any offer made can be withdrawn. I have on the table a proposition that I can happily accept. I do not want to lose it. I'll stick with it...a bird in the hand..." You were very wise; you closed when you had an acceptable offer on the table. If you are tempted to do an OliveTwist and ask for more remember the following Aesop Fable. A camel was walking happily in the desert. Into his sight came a bull with a fine set of horns. He was fascinated, then envious and decided that he must have a set for himself. In the evening he called on Zeus and asked if he could be given horns. Zeus became very cross and said that the camel should be satisfied with what he possessed. He must not be jealous or greedy. Zeus would not give the camel horns and, to teach him a lesson, reduced the size of the camel's ears. The moral is this - the camel wanted more, but lost some of what he already possessed because of his stupid jealousy and greed. It is the same with negotiators, when they have what has been sought close (accept) before it goes away.

To end this chapter let us get a little depressed, although as a salesperson you are advised never to do so. Just for a minute or so let us break that rule. The negotiations have broken down. All has failed. The collection of six 1841 Naval cutlasses which you could have sold for a very nice profit in your showrooms have been sold to another dealer. You dillied and dallied and lost the way whilst the successful dealer knew exactly what he wanted and immediately purchased. You are gutted and very depressed. An experienced salesperson would soon throw off the blues and happily bounce back. What else is there constructive to do? There is always tomorrow, always another deal around the corner. You have learned all that from experience. Look back over the negotiations where it all went wrong. How could you have improved your actions so as to successfully purchase those cutlasses? Why did you dilly and dally? Work out improvements so that you do not make the same mistake again. Then, forget about the cutlasses they are history. Get cracking and look for the next deal. Forget the "If only..." and move on. To slightly misquote a well-known motto - Nothing happens after a failure unless YOU make it.

At the start of my career I was employed as a property negotiator and one of the drawbacks of that employment is that sales agreed, subject to formal contract, do not always proceed to completion. As we say in the profession sales fall through. In my early days I was utterly depressed when I had a fall through. I soon realised that it was not all doom and gloom. I had a property owner who had just lost a sale and was anxious to find another buyer. That was a great opportunity never to be missed. A useful suggestion - after a setback there is always a comeback. Make sure that you snap out of the gloom following a failure and create the next opportunity.

A TIP ON SURVIVAL

AS YOU GAIN IN EXPERIENCE YOU WILL BE CONVINCED THAT ALL THOSE TRICKS THAT YOU EMPLOY AGAINST COMPETITORS WILL BE WINNERS. DO NOT BE FOOLED. MOST OF YOUR RIVALS KNOW THE SAME TRICKS AND CONSIDER THAT THEY ARE FAR MORE SKILFUL AT THEIR JOB THAN YOU. A WISE THOUGHT TO ALWAYS KEEP YOU ON YOUR TOES –

ALL NEGOTIATORS THAT YOU MEET ARE FIRST-CLASS

5

HOW TO WIN EVERYDAY ACTIONS

This chapter is devoted to difficult questions that often arise when negotiating. There are many different ways of solving a problem and until the problem is solved who knows which solution is the correct one? With your experience of negotiating you will soon realise the most apt solution to a problem as it come to light.

A TYPE OF DIFFICULT QUESTION

As you sit down in a competitor's office he snaps, "So, you want to buy a quantity of our exceptional sparking plugs?" Without any further ado he continues, "Our plugs are the best in the business and we can't be beaten on price. Only yesterday we sold two hundred and fifty thousand at our asking price to one of the leading garage chains in the UK. They realise their quality, their reliability…" The rant continues. The question is this - how do you stop the flow so that you can say a few words?

BACKGROUND INFORMATION:

This verbal bully has no manners. He is a typical greedy bully who is only concerned with himself and his own affairs to the exclusion of everything else. A type often met.

ADVICE:

This seller seems nervous and anxious to get the sales patter out of the way. He goes straight in, feet first. Let him talk as you might hear something of use. Sooner or later he has to pause. Then, step in before he starts up again. You see (that is, hear) an opportunity - grab it. Remain calm and be reasonable. Do not mention his bad-mannered display of verbosity. Talk about the subject under discussion. Do not break your talk and give him an opportunity to go rambling on. Get your buying patter over and make an offer for those sparking plugs. Then get him talking about your purchase and away from his show-off blab.

SOME OBSERVATIONS:

Assuming that this seller does not give you a chance to say a few words what should you do? You try and a wave of his hand brushes you aside. You may have to be a little rude and loudly talk whilst he is talking in an effort to be heard. Keep talking and he will stop. Immediately apologise for interrupting and say that you are anxious to say a few words. That low-key ticking off may make him feel a little guilty. He might even realise the error of his ways.

This seller is not only a verbal bully, he also boasts. That could be fatal to his cause. Question him about the sale of the two hundred and fifty thousand sparking plugs. Where they sold at the same price that you have been quoted? If not, why not? You are talking now, so make the most of his silence. Get him bewildered and his verbosity is unlikely to return.

If you are able to break into his verbal barrage on a positive note that will be a plus point. As an example, if he says, "Of course you know that our sparking plugs are of superior quality..." Grab the chance and exclaim, "Agreed..." He stops. He is happy to let you praise his wares. You continue, "...but the price is too high". He may be panicked away from quality and a price haggle is likely to take place. You have succeeded; you have broken into his tirade. A useful reminder - you went in on a positive note and immediately turned it into a negative. That is the ideal way to stop a boasting and aggressive bully who seems unstoppable.

As indicated above a verbal bully may say a few words that give a guide to his real feelings. You may get a glance of the real everyday him. It is always worth a careful listen before you try to shut him up. The most careful person can accidently say just a little too much. A useful suggestion - it is repeated that listening is a vital part of profitable negotiating. That is an element of negotiating that is so often overlooked.

A TYPE OF DIFFICULT QUESTION

You run a high-class antique gallery and have for sale a Kutani Gourd vase by Onokiln dated 1850. Business is very slow and prices (values) are tending to fall. You paid £175 for the vase and, as you urgently require cash, are marketing the vase at the same price. Unfortunately a similar vase sold at a London auction yesterday for only £125. A caller is inspecting the vase. He is known to you and he is not thought to be a professional - but you are not sure. What should be your sales patter to encourage a sale?

BACKGROUND INFORMATION:

Your vase is in mint condition. The London auctioneers were not helpful when you telephoned. Their representative *"thought"* that the sold vase was *"in quite good condition"* but was not certain. The auction catalogue did not describe the condition of the vase. You must sell your vase before the auction price becomes common knowledge.

ADVICE:

You have an obvious weakness in that a similar vase has just been sold at public auction at a lower price that you purchased yours. An auction sale well and truly tests the market and the values of sold items. Auction prices travel fast around the antique world and knowledgeable collectors are very soon au fait with the latest prices. An urgent sale is essential.

Your patter to a viewer must be based on any advantage that you possess. You do have a plus point that should be used. Your vase is in mint condition - a feature sought by collectors. No one can disagree with that fact - it is in the gallery to be inspected. Your viewer is unlikely to have seen the auctioned vase so is unable to compare the two vases. It cannot be convincingly argued that the sold vase was in mint condition. In fact, as it was not so described in the catalogue it is odds on that it was not so; also, the auctioneer`s representative did not give that impression. You cannot be sure that the viewer of your vase is not a professional, so to be safe keep your sales patter away from price and emphasis the mint condition.

If the viewer mentions the auctioned vase ask if he inspected it. If not, tell him that you were told by the auctioneer`s representative he *"thought"* (stress that word) that the vase was "in quite good condition". If he seems to doubt that suggest he telephones the auctioneers and hears their comments direct.

If the viewer does not mention the auction it can be safely assumed that he has no knowledge of the lower price obtained. Even so, keep your patter on the condition and, if necessary, to obtain a close drop the price. You have a prospective purchaser in front of you who does not know of the auction price. Grab the opportunity to rid yourself of a losing article. Any port in a storm...

SOME OBSERVATIONS:

You may consider that the above answer suggests that you break the rule that a weakness must be immediately exposed. You are not correct. You do not have a weakness until either a viewer knows and quotes the auction price or that fact is so well-known that you can safely assume that it is known to all likely buyers. In both events you must not forget the plus point - the mint condition of your vase versus the unknown true condition of the auctioned one.

A TYPE OF DIFFICULT QUESTION

After a long tedious negotiation with a truly tough negotiator you are given this ultimatum - As I told you I have another person keen on buying who will not wait much longer. You have until twelve noon tomorrow to conclude a deal at £6,750. Immediately after that I will sell to the other person". Which approach would you adopt - (a) Close the deal at £6,750? (b) Say go to Hell and walk away? (c) Say, "That's OK. Ring me if that other person doesn't buy?"

BACKGROUND INFORMATION:

Although you are an experienced negotiator you detest being put on the spot by an ultimatum. You always want to tell the ultimatum giver what you think of him. However, you are now more mature and less ill-tempered. In this case you cannot make up your mind whether or not you want to pay over your last bid of £6,250 for the goods. You hesitate. It seems that the ultimatum is a very weak one. Why is the competitor willing to wait until tomorrow when he has another buyer today? I wonder...?

ADVICE:

Would you be happy to pay £6,750? If so, is it worth arguing anymore? That other buyer may exist? Put your pride away, select (a) and do a deal. Or, if a true gambler, would a split-the-difference gambit help you to save a few pounds? But beware; the competitor may walk away to his other (real?) buyer.

Alternatively, assume that your last bid was £5,750. Are you so far from an agreement that you are rapidly losing interest in his goods? Then, select (c). However, you may consider one last fling was worthwhile. Offer to split-the-difference at ££6,250 - but, of course, only do that if the middle price suits you. If your proposal is refused and his ultimatum price is not modified put the ball in his court and adopt (c). Then, you can reconsider whether or not you want to purchase the goods and at what price if he comes back to you.

SOME OBSERVATIONS:

Never do a (b) even if you are at the end of your tether. It will sour any future relationship.

The ultimatum giver in this example may be a gambler (taking a calculated risk), a deceiver (there is no other buyer) or a good negotiator (sensing that you have weakened and are likely to accept the ultimatum terms). You will be watching him, like a hawk watches his potential prey, endeavouring to get a clue to which of the three attributes apply. This is an excellent example which vividly illustrates that salesmanship is a constant battle of wits and of gambles.

A TYPE OF DIFFICULT QUESTION

You are endeavouring to sell your car for £21,500. Within a minute or two of viewing a viewer puts forward a split-the-different proposal. The viewer came right out of the blue with, "I consider that the car is worth £17,500. Why don't we split-the-difference at £19,500?" You are taken by surprise. You consider that the car is worth £19,000 and that is the lowest price that you are prepared to accept. The offer that you have is £500 over that lower figure - and you did not have to negotiate to receive it. What should you do? A tricky question; close or...?

BACKGROUND INFORMATION:

At the back of your mind you admire the viewer. A man of action. You are keen to sell the car. It is only in "so-so" condition but it did pass the MOT two weeks ago. The money from the sale will help to pay off the bridging loan on your new car. The split-the-difference offer is tempting.

ADVICE:

This prospective buyer is either a superbly shrewd cookie who has immediately detected that you seek a quick deal or a poor negotiator whose only known tactic is to attempt to split down the middle. You judge the former. He is attempting to jump you into an immediate decision. You hesitate - why is he offering £2,000 more than what he says the car is worth? Perhaps not such a smooth cookie. As with all other answers there is not just one correct one; there are alternatives. It depends on the circumstances of both parties. In this example you are very keen to sell; the offer is £500 over what you were prepared to accept. You are a steady type, not a gambler, one who never seeks the last drop from any deal. OK, you are content with the offer and accept. Yet, you are human and leave the scene wondering whether you could have obtained a few more pounds.

SOME OBSERVATIONS:

If you had been a person who was willing to take a risk to try for a few more pounds the ideal ploy would be a split-the-difference offer. You have not offered to reduce the asking price. So, the halfway bid would be £20,500. Well worth a try as you would still have £1,500 in hand. But, he may walk away. Who knows, fictitious characters never reveal their innermost secrets!

A TYPE OF DIFFICULT QUESTION

During negotiations to sell your bungalow you make an untrue statement - in fact, you told a deliberate and nasty lie. The viewer was an annoying person asking very stupid questions, making silly disparaging remarks about the fittings in both the kitchen and bathroom, the decorations in the lounge, et al. You had tried to be pleasant as you are anxious to sell but finally you snapped. The difficult question asked was, "Have you good neighbours?" You replied, "Yes, very good, we have no complaints". In reality the adjoining semi-detached house is occupied by a couple and three dogs who are "neighbours from Hell". Quite suitable for inclusion in a TV programme. The three dogs bark incessantly, the radio and TV blare out until two o'clock in the morning. They only consider themselves and carry on as though they owned the road. That was the only reason that you wished to move. Whilst viewing was taking place all was quiet as the couple and the three dogs were out for a walk. Immediate after you made that statement you realised that it should not have been uttered. The difficult question is this - what should you do now?

BACKGROUND INFORMATION:

You are to a certain extent happy and feel that you have taken a little revenge on that annoying viewer. But, you wonder, have I acted illegally? Should I repent now and say that I had made a blunder? Whilst you are cogitating the viewer seems pleased to describe the central heating system as being "out of the ark". Utter cheek. Without any further doubt you decide not to admit your blunder. If he buys let him find out about the neighbours. That will serve him right.

ADVICE:

There is only one answer to that question. You must correct that deliberate lie before the viewer leaves the bungalow. That is a difficult exercise. You quite clearly stated that the neighbours were good neighbours and added for good measure, "...we have no complaints". A lie! On reflection that was an appalling answer to give. Whether you like it or not the lie has to be faced and corrected. Salespersons, negotiators and all dealers must never lie; it can lead to real trouble, legal cases and so on.

When you admit to the viewer that you have lied you must be totally honest. To be otherwise would compound your dilemma. Consider tackling the unpleasant task by commenting on both neighbours. Say, "Oh, about our neighbours. Bill and Jane are really nice. We often meet up for tea. The others are, to be honest, somewhat noisy". Will that answer suffice?...but you haven`t been totally honest, have you? You have put the viewer on limited notice that one set of neighbours are not as originally stated. You avoided saying that the noisy pair is in the bungalow attached to yours...and what about the dogs? A wise viewer would ask further questions about "noisy neighbours". As a potential seller do you consider that you have been perfectly clear and honest?

SOME OBSERVATIONS:

The following remarks apply to all buyers and sellers. It is so easy to say that you should not give way to an impulse and utter a wildly misleading statement. However, when about to strike a deal a seller can get carried away. He wants to close and can sometimes be a little reckless. Relating to the example given above. Firstly, you lied and by doing so could be in deep legal trouble. Whether or not that is so, you lied and that breaches all the rules of good salesmanship. Secondly, why did you lie? Purely and simply because you disliked the annoying viewer. Never do or say anything when negotiating just to even the score or to take revenge. You can be as competitive as you like, that is fair enough. You like the guy; you hate the guy - again that is fair enough. But it must not have any bearing on your negotiating tactics or your temper. It is said that you must treat your enemy as you would a friend. Your enemy deserves better than that! Anyhow, you must get the message loud and clear - always adopt a friendly attitude and without any doubt, always be truthful.

A useful suggestion - it is difficult, unpleasant and embarrassing to have to correct a lie or a mistake. When doing so you must tread carefully. You are admitting to have said or done something that a competitor could use against you. As stated, the correction must be honest and clear, yet there is still room for a little (legal) disguise so that the damage can be limited. The lesson is so obvious - do not lie. That is not as easy to achieve as it sounds for in the heat of the moment the best laid plans can come unstuck. Hence, it may be necessary to use a second line of defence as described but that is not telling the full story.

A TYPE OF DIFFICULT QUESTION

The opposite situation arises as that in the last question. The competitor has made a mistake - not told a lie. You are attempting to sell twelve thousand water cisterns. As one lot you ask £125,000. That is, £10.42p each. After frantic use of his calculator a possible buyer says, "You are asking £9.50p for each cistern (Comment - Either his calculator is broken or he doesn`t know how to use it). That`s a bit over value. I`ll give you £8.50p each, a total of £102,000. Sorry, can`t do any better". You quickly check on your calculator. Your figures are correct; his figure per cistern is hopelessly wrong. How do you break the bad news to him?

BACKGROUND INFORMATION:

You purchased the cisterns some nine months ago and it is proving difficult to resell in one lot. Each cost £9.00 and you had hoped to resell for at least £10.00 each in one lot. However, you now want rid of them and would accept £9.25p each in one lot, a total of £111,000. No way will you accept £102,000. The basis of the offer is wrong.

ADVICE:

Here we deal with the opposite state of affairs that were examined in the last question. This being the case, your gloom is replaced with glee and you can start having some fun. In this question the competitor`s mistake has lowered his offer; he is working on incorrect information which arises from his own blunder.

The potential buyer - or, his calculator - has calculated wrongly. He says the asking price is £9.50p each, whereas it is £10.42p. It is quite easy to correct that mistake. Do it in a humorous manner. Offer to lend him your calculator. Or, say, "I may be wrong (Comment – A splendid way to start, although you know that you are right). Did you hit the incorrect key - or, did I on mine? I make the asking price £10.42p each. Goodness me, they are realistically priced at that figure". Whilst the mistake is being corrected you keep up your sales talk. A good move. Keep pushing and praising your goods. He has another go at his calculator and you are in agreement; he reconsiders his offer.

A word of caution - do not let your competitor bring back into the negotiations the low price of £9.50p for each cistern. If it is referred to say, "Sorry, but that figure has no relevance whatsoever. It was a wrong figure resulting from a miss calculation". You were wise; you did not mention that it arose from a mistake that he made. If he is difficult and clings to the wrong figure you may have to be ruthless and rub home that the error was made by him and that both of you have already agreed the correct figure.

SOME OBSERVATIONS:

Remember that a mistake by a competitor may be a genuine one or made to mislead or deceive you. In this question it was a genuine mistake - as far as we know! It is a sound exercise to deal with both genuine and deliberate mistakes in the same way. Always be friendly. For example, "Sorry, but I can`t quite agree..." or, "I`m not with you on that one..." Give the competitor the opportunity of correcting his own mistake. Draw his attention to it as something you cannot quite understand. A little humour will often help. It must not be personal, just a little light humour or wit. When the mistake is admitted keep being friendly and helpful by saying, "Sorry to point that out. It didn't seem quite right to me".

It may be that a competitor will not admit to a mistake and sticks to his guns. The ball is firmly back in your court. At that stage you must be a lot tougher but still be friendly and helpful. Say, "Sorry (Comment - You are always being sorry. That shows that you are friendly and uncomfortable about pointing out his error), do you mind if we go over that again as I still can't quite understand it". That shows that you will not be put off the scent. Eventually he will be as keen to correct the mistake a you are to expose it.

Because of your friendly and helpful manner he will want to put the mistake to sleep as quickly as possible. He will wonder if you are trying to help him or yourself. A useful reminder - notice how you are not directly pointing out a mistake - you cannot quite understand what he is saying, Will he, please, explain further? You are asking for his help. He will soon get the message.

Remember - always be sorry; never unsympathetic

A TYPE OF DIFFICULT QUESTION

You are eager to purchase a pair of antique gates for your driveway at your home. In the antique dealer's yard they are priced at £1,200. Having seen a number of pairs of gates on offer by other dealers you feel that £1,200 is an over valuation. Your wife likes the gates and is pushing you to purchase. You are adamant that there must be some reduction in price. You offer £1,000. The dealer will not budge. So, you increase to £1,050 and state that that is your top bid. Still, the owner will not budge and repeats that £1,200 is the price - sorry but no reduction. On principle you are determined to obtain some reduction. What should your next move be?

BACKGROUND INFORMATION:

There is little between you - only £150 and that seems a small sum for which to lose the gates as both your wife and yourself like them. But to you, as a good negotiator, it is always satisfying to negotiate a reduction - even a small on. If you walk away you will be dejected if tomorrow you return to the yard and the gates have been sold.

ADVICE:

The owner of the gates will not drop a penny. The price is £1,200 and that is final. A typical example of a closed mind, although he may be convinced that he is offering superb value. To you it is imperative that you get a reduction; it is all about being a first-class negotiator who is rarely beaten - and, of course, your wife is watching the dual between another dealer and yourself! You consider walking away; but he seems so sure that £1,200 is the price that he is unlikely to stop you. The gap is only £150; who can so accurately value antique gates? How, without losing face, how can you bridge that gap? The answer is to try a split-the-difference ploy. Say, "Look, we are so close. You want to sell and I want to buy. I've offered £1,050. You still stand at the original asking price of £1,200. Let's meet halfway - I'll come right up to £1,125. That sounds fair to me. Don't you agree?"

If the seller is so closed that he turns down the offer you will have to pay the full price or walk away. If you walk away say that the £1,125 offer still stands. As always walk slowly. He may change his mind - if not, you may change yours.

SOME OBSERVATIONS:

A real closed mind is so hard to open. This owner knew that you were unlikely to lose the gates for only £75 - he was right; you bought them. Neither the owner nor yourself made the final decision. It was made by your wife.

The dealer was a superb negotiator. Right from the start he realised that your wife loved the gates and was determined to persuade you to buy. The dealer worked on that knowledge; although his work was only standing firm and waiting. How did you hope to win against two such determined persons? There is a lesson to learn in that story - when selling to a couple furtively aim your sales patter at the lady.

A TYPE OF DIFFICULT QUESTIONS

It has been a long hard struggle during which you have been the person struggling. The fireplace that you seek to purchase is priced at £4,000. You first offered £2,800 and slowly increased to £3,500. The owner/builder had only taken £200 off the asking price as you said you would remove it from his yard. So, that was not a true reduction - it was his saving in cost of transport. You are of the firm opinion that £3,500 is its top value. You dig your toes in.

The owner is a talkative fellow and goes on about all the fireplaces that he has sold and this one is the finest of the lot. He explains that his company sells loads of building materials that come from properties that are demolished and normally offers on quoted prices are not accepted. You listen and the talkative fellow will not reduce the price. The question is this - have you any hope that a figure under £3,800 will be accepted?

BACKGROUND INFORMATION:

Lucky for you that the builder does not know the reason why you want to buy that particular fireplace. Your house is being modernised and the builder cannot proceed with the work in the lounge until you have acquired a new fireplace. There is one big plus point with the fireplace that you are trying to purchase. It is not a standard size and fits into the abnormal size breast in your lounge. That will save much work, time and money. Also, the abnormal size may put off other possible purchasers. However, the dealer must not know of your possible saving as he may well increase the asking price.

ADVICE:

You urgently require a fireplace and this one is ideal. You have increased your offer by £700, whereas the builder has only reduced by £200 and that is a saving to him. As a keen negotiator you have listened to his incessant chatter and have heard, "and *normally* we don't take offers". Is that a sign that he is weakening a just a little? That is what you like to hear. He talks on and there is no mention of acceptance of a lower price. You strongly confirm a firm bid of £3,500 and that you have the cash with you and state that is your final offer. No acceptance. You cogitate. If you walk away and return tomorrow the fireplace may be sold elsewhere. The builder is getting browned off and says, "That's my final price - £3,800 - it's up to you, take it or leave it. Sorry, I must leave you and get on with my work". As a final throw of the dice you offer to split-the-difference; even a saving of £150 will help your stretched finances. Who won; who knows? The seller held the ace although he did not know how anxious the prospective buyer was to buy the odd size fireplace.

SOME OBSERVATIONS:

If you walk away it is a good ploy to return in a day or so to see if the item is still on offer for sale. You must adopt a casual and couldn't careless attitude. You do not mention that fireplace; you ask if there are any similar fireplaces for sale. Suddenly you notice the fireplace that you did not buy. "Oh, not yet sold! I thought that you would sell that without any trouble, it being the best fireplace that you ever had". Who is in the strongest negotiating position? The builder who has an unsold fireplace on his hands, yet is convinced that you have returned to buy? Or you seeing that the fireplace is still unsold and knowing (hoping) that an odd - size fireplace is not easy to sell?

A TYPE OF DIFFICULT QUESTION

You are one of the salesmen in a firm. Over the last six months your personal sales have badly fallen away. During the last four week period sales were nearly non-existent yet the other salesmen were selling well. On receipt of the figures the Sales Director demotes you to a junior salesman, reduces your commission rate, rates you a smaller car and a reduced expenses allowance. The question is this - what do you do to improve sales so that you gain your lost status?

BACKGROUND INFORMATION:

During the last few weeks you realised that sales had been under the usual target. You are extremely worried and sensed that you had lost your usual confidence. Until the Sales Director disclosed the actual figures you did not realise that your sales were so dramatically down on the same period last year. You are shocked.

ADVICE:

For the next few evenings you do not watch TV. You go back over some of the failed calls you made. You look for errors made and for opportunities not grabbed. You isolate your weak points. You consider in detail each one and decide how you should have acted. Were you in too much of a hurry? Did you try to see too many customers and, hence, each individual one did not get the attention deserved? Did you not push quality and value? You are likely to find a repetition of errors in some calls. A persistent error may have been your downfall. Do not let it happen again. A useful suggestion -

when in trouble take the time to identify errors and seek out remedies. Play less golf. An error eradicated is experience truly gained.

<u>SOME OBSERVATIONS</u>:

It will be advantageous to look back at the interview with the Sales Director.

A snap decision to leave the firm would have been wrong. For both your own esteem and for your future, it must be proved that set-backs can be overcome. Do not run away as not facing bad times will become a habit. Fight the problem head on. When you are back in full swing examine the past and recap on the way that it worked out. You would have learnt some worthwhile lessons which will be so helpful when the next set-back comes along. Do not kid yourself, set-backs come along when not expected; just like thunder storms on a lovely summer`s day.

At the meeting it was not an iota of use pleading for your existing position to be retained. Why should the boss reverse a decision just because you asked him too? There was no alternative; you had to agree that your sales were bad. You reminded him that in the past you had sold well. You said, "You`re right to demote me. That`s fair. I ask you, please, to be fair to me. Give me three months to prove my worth. Then, if I produce good figures - I am sure that I will - consider giving me back the monetary considerations that you have just taken away. Don`t promote me on three month`s figures as I`ll get back my lost status on merit.".

Having been given three months to improve you must immediately get down to work. Time flashes by and you do not want to be beaten by time. There is no time to wallow in gloom and self-pity. You cannot afford such luxuries. Without doubt, you are on your way back. Remember that only one person can complete your recovery - **YOU**. So, in the final analysis you only have yourself to rely on, other persons may have ideas that are not in your interest.

A TYPE OF DIFFICULT QUESTION

You are a negotiator with a well-known firm of estate agents. You have had a very good record of sales over a ten year period. Sadly, you have hit a bad patch. In the four weeks now being reviewed you sold, subject to contract, six properties. In itself that is a poor performance but four of those sales did not proceed to completion. Only two sales earned the firm and yourself some real hard cash. You are especially upset as one of the abortive sales was a high-class luxury mansion which would have produced a colossal fee. You sit back in your office chair and gloomily gaze out of the window. The question is this - what should be your recovery plan?

BACKGROUND INFORMATION:

All salespersons have periods when likely sales do not proceed to completion. This particularly applies to those who negotiate properties as sales agreed, subject to contract, may or may not become real fee earners. Take that from one who knows from (very) bitter experience. Your recent experience is somewhat unusual and very upsetting for you. The question is this - why are your sales so poor and why do many agreed sales not proceed to completion?

ADVICE:

You, as an estate agent's negotiator are in an entirely different situation to the salesman in the preceding question. He is working for a firm and has their goods to sell. You have a register of properties for sale of varying sizes, prices and locations and can, to a certain (limited) degree, pick and choose the properties that you endeavour to sell across the entire register. Even so, you should concentrate your efforts on the most saleable properties. I know from experience that it can be worked that way.

As with virtually all private jobs there are two goals to satisfy. Firstly, to earn money for the firm. That is, to do enough business to cover the cost of employing you and an excess towards the firm's expense, profit, et al. Secondly, you must personally earn sufficient money to keep your family. Hence, you cannot continue for any length of time with poor sales figures. You have no time to spare or waste - too much depends on you and your earnings. You have no alternative, you must take immediate action. Look at your last performances as required of the salesman in the last question. In particular ascertain from the firms' sales the type and price of properties that are selling. Immediately concentrate, as far as is possible, on that type and price of property. You may have to follow that lead rather than the pick and choose method.

There is an interesting lesson to be learnt from this unfortunate negotiator. It is this - all salespersons must make sure that their sales are properly closed. Some salespersons, particularly those who deal with property, have to agree sales that are subject to contract and other conditions. Hence, sales are generally not binding and rely on solicitors to take the sales to completion.

Be that as it may, did you look close enough at the prospective purchaser's finance so as to ensure that any mortgage was obtainable? If not, you were kidding yourself and hoping that all was well. Did you research sufficiently when told that the prospective purchaser had to sell his own house to finance the purchase of his new home? Again, if not you were kidding yourself and just hoping that the house would be sold. Were you too keen for a sale (some commission) that you overlooked these and other essential details? The lesson is this - only go to a conditional close if you are truly satisfied that all conditions are reasonable and can be met. Make sure that all conditions are clearly stated, an ambiguous condition may make the deal null and void. Do not let a competitor impose a condition that is unreasonable.

SOME OBSERVATIONS:

A summary - only agree a sale subject to a condition that is reasonable and you are sure - that is, as sure as you can be - that it can be met. Also, impose a strict timetable. Thereafter, keep in touch with the deal and do not rest until the condition has been met and the matter finalised. Only then will some cash come your way.

THOSE ARE SUGGESTED SOLUTIONS TO SOME DIFFICULT QUESTIONS. YOU WILL REALISE THAT IN REAL LIFE THE FUTURE IS RARELY PREDICTABLE. THESE ANSWERS ARE TO HELP YOU TO UNRAVEL THE PROBLEMS THAT ARISE IN MOST NEGOTIATIONS AND, ALSO, TO ILLUSTRATE THE SUDDEN TWISTS AND TURNS OF SALESMANSHIP. THAT IS WHY **A SALESPERSON SHOULD NEVER RELAX AND LOWER HIS GUARD.**

6

HOW DO YOU ANSWER THAT UNANSWERABLE QUESTION?

All salespersons are asked questions that are nearly impossible to answer without in some way divulging information that will completely or partially destroy their own line of reasoning. Sometimes the questions are posed by an aggressive competitor who is keen to display his superior negotiating powers. But tread cautiously for such questions are invariably asked to capture an advantage. There is no hiding place - you cannot remain silent. Some examples of this type of question are listed below. The answers are my suggestions and, of course, you may have other ideas and different answers. The plan behind this exercise is to help you answer, partially answer or intelligently sidestep this type of (nearly) unanswerable question. A first thought - it is imperative not to be condemned out of your own mouth.

Do remember that on paper with no one to shoot down your answer it is so easy to give a reply that will destroy the questioner. If you consider that it might be an easy exercise in the real world you must remove the blinkers right now. When negotiating you will be endeavouring to answer difficult questions from a person determined to drag facts and figures from you. He, like you, depends for his daily bread on being a top notch negotiator. You have no option, you must respond in some intelligent way. The following awkward questions and answers will help to prepare you for the clash with equally - and better - skilled operators.

There are far more prickly questions than those mentioned below. The idea of this chapter is to illustrate that you can settle the score by using a little cunning. The questioner is doing his utmost to catch you off guard, Do not be frightened of any question. Even so, for a few seconds you do not know how to reply. Do not let it be seen that that you are lost for words. Occasionally, you have to directly face a questioner and, whilst considering what to say or do, smile and make a semi-humorous remark like, "That's a silly question - you don't want a silly answer, do you?" That is a remark meaning very little, but as the questioner replies it will give you a little more time to collect your thoughts.

AN UNANSWERABLE QUESTION

A QUESTION OF A VULGAR OR OFFENSIVE - Let us dispose of any questions that are truly offensive. Such questions may be of a personal nature, contain vulgar, rude or foul language, be racial, be of a religious nature, et al. You will know the questions that come within that category. The most damaging defence is to answer in the same manner. Beware, that would cause a nasty controversy...and that will get you nowhere. You may feel that it is pointless trying to deal with such an obnoxious individual who uses such vile methods. When such an occasion arises you will have to decide whether to stand and reason or walk away - it will depend on the circumstances at the time. One important influence will be how keen you are to do that particular business with him. If you are keen you may be prepared to put up with some aggressive behaviour; but never take extreme aggressive behaviour. In except the very special cases you should be able to find the business elsewhere in more acceptable circumstances. If you walk away make it absolutely clear why you are doing so.

So, if you are keen to do the business you must engage with that unpleasant character, despite the fact that his attitude has made you dislike him. His actions have ruined his image. Sadly, beggars cannot be choosers and despite his behaviour you must continue to sell yourself as a decent guy. I have found that the best way is to assume and show that under all that aggression he is a reasonable person. A difficult activity; nevertheless necessary. You say, "Come on, Mr Brown, you are too decent a person to mean that. Let's be reasonable..." or, "I didn't expect to start our meeting on that level. Let's start again and be polite to each other..." If he does not calm down and be reasonable you will have to be more forthright. "I am sorry to say that I am not happy hearing such language at a business meeting. If we cannot continue in a proper business-like manner I will have to leave this meeting. I will be disappointed if I have to do that". These quotations may be altered to suit the circumstances of each negotiation. I have found that such comments often calm a competitor; and on occasions I have received an apology. Isn`t that approach/defence better than entering into a profitless slanging match?

AN UNANSWERABLE QUESTION

IN ANSWER TO A BOAST THAT YOU MADE THAT THERE ARE SEVERAL POTENTIAL BUYERS INTERESTED IN YOUR GOODS. THE QUESTION IS, "IF THAT IS SO WHY ARE YOU TRYING SO HARD TO SELL THEM TO ME?"

You had forgotten one of the most important principles of salesmanship and had jumped in with, "I have numerous other prospective purchasers interested..." The viewer snapped back the quoted question above. Immediately you realised that "...the numerous other prospective buyers..." have inspected and "will contact you later..." Hardly viewers that you should boast about. In truth, there is not any real competition, not one of those viewers showed real firm interest. The present viewer senses that he has no real competition. Your possible answer, "You are an expert in the antique world (Comment - Flattery may get you somewhere) and know that viewers call, inspect and go away to think about it and call back with a decision later. Few people buy on the first visit". (Comment - You know that if your antique desk had been in first-class condition the first viewer would have snapped it up). I expect some calls later in the day". A poor answer. A situation made by you has forced you to reply in that down beat tone. A useful suggestion - keep quiet unless you have something really positive to say that will strengthen your cause.

You could have avoided this question by not making that silly boast. It is better to remain quiet and let the competitor make the moves. The goods are yours and the price has been quoted so do not jump in feet first and brag - that will, as seen in the last paragraph, get you into trouble.

AN UNANSWERABLE QUESTION

YOU HAVE BEEN TRYING TO SELL YOUR HOUSE FOR MANY MONTHS. A VIEWER ASKS, "WHY IT IS STILL UNSOLD?"

Your house has been on the market for seven months. It is proving very difficult to sell. At last a viewer makes an offer some way below the already reduced asking price. After some tough haggling the highest bid is still £273,500; that is £16,500 below the asking price. A week goes by and you do not hear from the offerer; then out of the blue she calls and repeats her last made offer. She tries to bounce you into an acceptance with, "I know that the house has been in the market for over seven months and that other houses around here have sold quite quickly. Why is it still unsold?" That difficult question goes straight to the jugular.

The honest answer is that although the first asking price was as advised by the estate agents it has been reduced twice to its present figure and yet those reductions produced no interest at all. You have no idea why it has not been sold - neither have the estate agents. Such a reply would put a viewer on guard. No one wants to buy a house that is going to be very difficult to sell in the future unless it was purchased at a bargain price that reflected its poor saleability. The lady who made the offer is cautious as her employers are likely to move her to another town within five years. Therefore, that honest answer may kill any chance of a sale. You dismiss being too honest and consider two alternatives.

Firstly, the (near) truth is that your new bungalow will be ready for occupation on the 1st of May - some ten weeks` time. Until now you were not worried that the house was unsold. However, you suddenly realised that time is flying and you must sell so as to finance the final payment to the builders. Therefore, a reduction in asking price is to attract a buyer. That is a fair answer as those circumstances do arise in the real world.

Secondly, a different approach - but not honest. You have been disappointed as two interested parties want to buy but neither has yet sold their own house. Sadly, both houses remain unsold and on the market. As your new bungalow will be ready in about ten week`s time the asking price has been reduced to attract a buyer.

The snag with both reasons is that the seller is exposed as one who has a very compelling reason to negotiate a quick sale. However, needs must be and the seller has placed himself in a difficult position. This is a case where his estate agents must use their negotiating powers to overcome a weakness.

There is much to learn from the above example. It is common sense that if a possible buyer knows that the goods have been for sale for a long time he will play on it...and why not? In his shoes every sharp negotiator would do likewise. The answer is that the seller must find a plausible reason to "wipe away the past". And the goods must be offered at today`s prices and on today`s conditions. The asking price must reflect that no one has snapped up the goods and it is pointless for the seller to continue offering his goods at yesterday`s prices. The bungalow owner`s possible two answers were reasonable. But, as seen, both revealed a weakness for the interested party to exploit.

To "wipe away the past" is not an easy exercise. It is there and potential purchasers will endeavour to benefit. As mentioned above, the owner must make sure that the asking prices of unsold goods are today`s realistic prices and not yesterday`s prices that have been sought and not obtained. If this is not done it will give possible buyers a field day when negotiating and putting forward an offer to an already self-defeated owner.

AN UNANSWERABLE QUESTION

WHEN SELLING YOUR HOUSE TWO QUESTIONS CAN CAUSE PROBLEMS (1) WHY ARE YOU MOVING? AND (2) HOW MUCH DID YOU PAY FOR IT?

Retaining our interest in the housing market as salespersons can learn many lessons from that source as it is, without doubt, the most active arena for both buying and selling. A rather tricky question is this, "You said that you purchased about a year ago. So, why are you on the move so soon?" The correct answer may well disclose a defect in the house or problems with a neighbour. A hint in one of those directions could be of great use to a clever negotiator. Your answer could be somewhat vague but it must not be a lie; that could lead to legal problems if the questioner purchased the house from you. Of course, if the problem was of a major one it would be dangerous to keep it from a viewer. Prospective purchasers do have surveys but that does not absolve the owner from the impact of giving wrong information. The honest answer may be that although the house has a certain defect - you name and describe the defect - the asking price reflects that flaw.

That is a lesson to be learnt when selling all goods with defects of some description - the price must reflect any imperfection and when a prospective purchaser asks he must be told the truth. There is no reason to lie if the price fully reflects the imperfections.

The next question is "...and how much did you pay for it?" Most viewers will know that recent sale prices can be seen on the Internet. So, in most cases the viewer will be able to tell the owner the price he paid! When the owner purchased the property some time ago the price is really irrelevant. Often the question is only asked to be nosey. A polite answer could be along these lines, "I purchased this house so long ago that the price I paid has no bearing whatsoever on a sale today. Of course, a sale will be at today`s price and that really is the only figure to talk about now".

When selling any type of property and a possible buyer talks about yesterday`s prices it is reasonable to say, "As you will appreciate prices go up and prices go down - that is the nature of all markets. That is an interesting theory but sales are made on today`s prices."

AN UNANSWERABLE QUESTION

WHEN YOU ARE FULLY CONSCIOUS THAT YOUR OWN GOODS ARE TOO EXPENSIVE

You are advertising a car for sale and after a general chat with a viewer he says, "I was offered a similar car only yesterday. It is a 2003 model, so yours is two years older; it has clocked 5,359 miles less. The price is slightly lower although the owner led me to believe that a near offer might be accepted. Isn`t your car overpriced?" You realise that if the viewer is telling the truth the answer is "yes". To be truthful, you knew that it was overpriced before he viewed. You must fight back, be firm and emphasise that it is not possible for you to comment on a car that you have not seen. Following that observation there are two possible lines of attack:

Firstly, you must be frank. You must try to undermine his rosy view of the competing car. You ask questions like these - "How do conditions compare?", "Has it always been serviced and maintained in line with the maker`s recommendations - as mine has?", "Has it been kept in a garage overnight? Mine is never exposed to the night air", "Has it four new tyres like mine?" and so on. How, you plead, can I compare it with mine? Mine is here. Thoroughly inspect it and let`s take it for a road test". You must help the viewer in every respect but you cannot comment on a car you have not seen. You can ask questions but must not get involved in a dialogue which compares the visible with the invisible.

Secondly, this answer is said more in jest but it has a sting in its tail, "Take me to it". Now, that is a challenge. The viewer will huff and puff. Excuses will be made. You speak in jest again, "Does it really exist? Of course, I`m only joking for if it`s as good as you say It will be sold by now". The viewer will become uneasy. If the other car does not exist he will not know which way to turn; he will want to forget his ploy and bring the discussions back to the car that is being inspected.

A useful suggestion - do not argue that an object in front of you is better than an unseen one. It does not make any sense and that argument will never be truly won. Concentrate what can be seen by the competitor and yourself. Use every opportunity to praise, praise and praise again the visual object.

Thirdly, a simple reply could be, "It`s up to you; I haven`t seen the other car". Such a reply is not as helpful to you as the ones in the last paragraphs. It does little to aid the sale of your car. You realise that only tough positive negotiating wins the day. Nevertheless, that short sharp answer may jolt the viewer into a more realistic stance. You may have to use it if all else fails and he keeps harping on about that unseen car. Keep this suggestion in reserve.

AN UNANSWERABLE QUESTION

WHEN YOU ARE FACED WITH A TOUGH NEGOTIATOR WHO SAYS, "NO ONE IS BUYING THAT STUFF NOWADAYS".

Many dealers who are buying from the man in the street start their patter by saying that "No one is buying that stuff nowadays". After a pause is added, "Didn`t you know that?" This line of attack is, firstly, to depress the seller and, secondly, "...Didn`t you know..." puts the seller on the spot. If the answer is "no" the dealer will correct the seller`s ignorance by giving examples of similar goods which he recently turned down. The seller is on the losing side. If the answer is "yes" the seller has committed himself and is on the losing side. You just can`t win!

When faced with this question do not answer with a "yes" or "no". There are two ways of tackling it:

Firstly, you ignore the question and praise your goods and say that you have researched the market and are happy with the results. Your goods are priced to sell, warts and all. Ignore the difficult question and keep praising your goods and their value which, you repeat, truly reflects today`s market value.

Secondly, tackle the question with a little humour. Give a bright smile and say, "Do you always say that? Come on, you have pulled my leg; now let`s get down to some real business". I have been known to add "...then you can return to your villa in Bermuda". It is all done in good friendly humour.

Remember - do not let anyone depress you by claiming that market conditions are difficult and that no one is buying, et al. That is a typical dealer`s moan. You know the market as well as the next man - probably better. Hit back. Use a little wit. Smile and the competitor will smile with you.

AN UNANSWERABLE QUESTION

WHEN A COMPETITOR ASKS YOU TO DISCLOSE SOME CONFIDENTIAL FACTS RELATING TO ANOTHER PARTY INVOLVED IN THE DEAL

I was attempting to buy two adjacent houses on the sea front of a south coast town. They would be demolished and a small block of flats erected on the site. I agreed a price with owner A in a straightforward deal. Owner B was an entirely different kettle of fish. She admitted that she was keen to sell and move to be near her son. That was good news and a plus point for me proving that she was not a good negotiator. I knew that those two owners had quarrelled some years ago and had not spoken since. After a long and fruitless meeting with owner B she asked me the embarrassing question, "How much are you paying owner A?" Of course, it was not possible for me to answer that question. I explained that I was never at liberty to disclose another person`s business without their consent. I knew that there was no hope of getting consent from owner A as we had agreed a price on the strict understanding that I did not disclose it to owner B. I was pushed hard by owner B and I reasoned, "I know that you will appreciate (Comment - A good start as I was being kind to her) that it is not possible for me to discuss someone else`s business with another person. If it was the other way round I would not disclose your business to owner A. Don`t you agree that confidential business must remain confidential?" She did not agree when owner A was concerned and tried some devious ways to force me to give a guide. I was questioned, "Is it under…?", "Is it over…?" and so on. I praised her, "You are a good negotiator and I have to be on my guard. Nevertheless, in no circumstances whatsoever can I break a confidence…sorry, not even a clue". We parted on a friendly basis and it took two more meetings before we agreed a deal.

On other occasions I have been pushed very hard to disclose confidential information. In the last resort I suggest that the difficult question should be put directly to the other party for their consent to disclose. I do not ever recall that challenge being taken up.

A useful suggestion - make it an unbreakable rule never to disclose in any way confidential information. Giving it to any other person is just not done. Never give even a hint. Do remember that the person who receives confidential information from you will downgrade you in his estimation. You will not be trusted by that person. Therefore, you will have broken not one but two strict rules. Firstly, you have breached a confidence, which is a grave error. Secondly, you have caused someone to lose faith in you, which is a personal calamity.

AN UNANSWERABLE QUESTION

WHEN A POTENTIAL BUYER DISPUTES THE GENUINENESS OF THE ARTICLE YOU ARE SELLING AND REQUESTS, "WHO ADVISED YOU OF…"

You have for sale a beautiful carved walnut wall clock. You have been told that the maker was Fredrick Mauthe and that it is an early 20th century model. You are asking £300. You know very little about clocks and a friend has identified it as being a Fredrick Mauthe. The owner of a second-hand furniture shop is inspecting the clock. He frowns. You frown. He asks the difficult question, "Who advised you that this clock is a Fredrick Mauthe?" Your frown deepens, "Ah…a friend of mine". The expert gently breaks the bad news. "I`m am sorry to have to tell you that this is not a Mauthe. It`s less than five years old and was made in Germany. It is not a fake. It`s a good modern clock worth about £50". You struggle. "...but...my friend told me..." You had some doubts about your friend`s opinion and you decide that the second-hand furniture dealer is right. You strike a deal at £52.50p. It now resides in a collection of clocks by Fredrick Mauthe. The owner was pleased to give the second-hand dealer £1,000 for it.

There are many lessons to be learnt from that sad episode. You were robbed. The difficult question was a cunning trick question. It was made by a person who you thought (hoped) was a reputable expert on antiques and you accepted his advice. A local second-hand shop owner is unlikely to be the best person to give advice on a valuable clock - especially a crooked person! The moral is this - only take advice from a real independent expert. When you are not one hundred per cent sure of vital facts and figures when negotiating take advice from a known reputable and acknowledged expert on those items concerned. Never be shy of doing that.

A never to be forgotten observation - that unanswerable question may be asked with more than one objective in mind. The main object may be to deceive. As in this example, one question and two objectives. This shows that all salespersons must be constantly vigilant and never drop their guard for one moment.

AN UNANSWERABLE QUESTION

THIS IS THE SILLY QUESTION THAT SHOULD NEVER BE ASKED - "HOW MUCH WILL YOU ACCEPT?"

I have for sale a first edition of His Last Bow by Sir Arthur Conan Doyle. It is in excellent condition although it has been rebound. It has been valued at circa £1,000 and I am asking £1,150. A very talkative viewer asks that unanswerable question, "What price will you accept?" That stupid question always riles me and I want to reply, "Don`t expect me to do your work for you. Can`t you see the price that I am asking?" However, I hold my breath and try to remain calm. Sometimes I quote the asking price being the price that I will accept. Ask a silly question, you get a silly reply. A more detailed reply might be, "My asking price is £1,150. I have been advised that this first edition is valued at that price. It`s not a guess, it`s not a figure plucked from the air, it`s not a starting point, it's the value that an acknowledged expert has advised". Those sentiments can be altered to suit varying circumstances.

When a seller answers that question with a price it becomes in his mind a firm figure. Having given that price he is unlikely to reduce any further. So, the question may well have brought forth a reply to the questioner's detriment. Do not ask - negotiate.

At antique fairs it is custom to ask, "What's your best...?" When in Rome do as the Romans do...

As an aside, I do not like seeing "Price £5,000 **or offer**". Why add those last two words? Firstly, it means that the seller is unlikely to obtain £5,000 as offers are invited below that figure and interested parties will take him at his word and make offers. Secondly, it tells the reader that the owner has no or little confidence in the asking price. A useful suggestion, ask a price and leave it at that. Offers will be made even if not requested. A firm price will greatly assist your negotiating powers.

AN UNANSWERABLE QUESTION

A PERSON TRIES TO INTIMIDATE YOU BY GLOOMILY STATING THAT A BAD RECESSION/SLUMP IS AROUND THE CORNER. THEN, TREATING YOU LIKE A DIMWIT DROOLS, "DIDN'T YOU KNOW?"

When I was active in the property world buying and selling all types of properties I was constantly being told that, to quote Noel Coward, "There are bad times just around the corner". Rarely was it true; it was a ploy to depress both me and the price. I have a special motto/thought to remind me not to yield to that gloom and despondency. It is this - the worst rarely happens. I would respond to that gloomy prediction along these lines. "You may be right, you may be wrong. But looking at the market as it is there are no signs of a recession. The market is very active - more like a minor boom than a recession. I hear no talk of bad times ahead. It's up to you. Don't buy if it worries you. That's how confident I am of the market remaining active.". That sentiment can be altered to suit varying conditions.

Although that onslaught did not convince every competitor it did clear the air. The suggestion of a slump/recession left the agenda. Why was I warned of bad time only when I was selling - never when I was buying?

SALESMANSHIP - A SUMMARY

It is a difficult task to give a compressed summary of all the advice, ideas, suggestions, et al., mentioned in this first section. There are specific characteristics that every first-class salesperson must possess. These are all personal traits and enable his job to be undertaken in both a competent and profitable manner. These traits are the basis of his craft and will, therefore, form a useful summary at this end of this section.

A FIRST-CLASS SALESPERSON –

MUST...genuinely love his job. He who does not will seldom thrive. It must not be just a nine-to-five job. That is not good enough. A useful reminder - alongside my motto I put...**nothing comes without work.**

MUST...know that both selling and buying provide a valuable and useful service to the public, to his customers and to his firm. It gives him an interesting and varied career and adequate personal income.

MUST...be proud of and have confidence in the goods and/or services that he markets and the manner in which he conducts his business. He will know that he will not be able to sell successfully if he is ashamed of talking about or displaying his goods or services. He must be proud of his wares, their condition and their value.

MUST...know that the asking prices of his goods and/or services are about right and reflects their quality.

MUST...like meeting and talking to prospective buyers and sellers and keeping both past and present customers happy. That is his main contact with the marketplace; it is a vital aspect of his business life.

MUST...get a real thrill when a deal is completed.

MUST...know that he is first-class at his job. Always doing his very best to help customers and potential customers. He is always helpful, polite and friendly.

ARE YOU NOW A FIRST-CLASS SALESPERSON? TO ACCORD WITH ALL THOSE SEVEN VIRTUES MUST BE YOUR AIM. TAKEN TOGETHER THEY FORM A FIRM BASE ON WHICH TO BUILD A WORTHWHILE VOCATION. <u>NOTHING HAPPENS UNLESS YOU MAKE IT.</u>

<u>ON ADVERTISING</u>

7

INTRODUCTION TO ADVERTISING

There is an eight line poem which is of great interest to those who advertise. It brilliantly displays that those who advertise **and** require profitable results must say or do something to be either heard or seen above the crowd. The "homely hen" of the poem because of his cackle attracts attention and advertised his presence. The author of this splendid poem is unknown and it is, thus, attributed to "Anon". Here is the verse.

> **The cod fish lays ten thousand eggs,**
> **The homely hen lays one.**
> **The codfish never cackles**
> **to tell you what she`s done.**
> **So we scorn the codfish,**
> **While the humble hen we prize.**
> **Which only goes to show -**
> ## That it pays to advertise.

This section has two aims. Firstly, to give a straightforward and direct approach to advertising to those persons whose work involves the actual drafting of advertisements. That person will fully understand that his job and personal income rely on the drafting of money-earning displays. Please note the words "money-earning displays" for, in our context, those displays are the only grouping that matter. That advertiser cannot afford to fail. This section will reinforce the draftsman`s existing talents. Secondly, it will assist the novice to fully understand the functions of advertising and to become a good draftsman. Those advantages will remain with him throughout his career. Additionally, it will convince him that salesmanship and advertising form the basis of all good and profitable business.

There are both legal and moral reasons why honesty in advertising is the best and only policy. In nearly all countries there is legislation to protect consumers and it is essential that you know and abide by the law when you advertise. If there is any element of doubt whatsoever consult your lawyers. Advertising, like all walks of life, has a few bad exponents who bring it into disrepute. Good taste and a sense of fair play have to be maintained without stifling the competitive and pioneering spirit. The maintenance of standards does not seriously restrict the draftsman; on the contrary, it offers the challenge of producing well-mannered displays which are a credit to the advertiser and to advertising generally.

Therefore, your first vital lesson is to make sure that all your displays are legal and decent (well-mannered) for that is the only way to attract and keep profitable business.

The following three observations will illustrate just how important advertising is to you and your firm.

Firstly, advertising and marketing are both emotive subjects. Both are much abused by those who do not really understand their true functions. Nevertheless, they are the life blood of all business and trade and the prerequisite to the entire negotiating process. Without advertising there would be much less business transacted as sellers and buyers could not so easily locate each other. Consider this question - What happens when you do not advertise? The only answer is - very little or, more likely, nothing. It follows that you must advertise and from that comment you must learn to draft and display advertisements that will produce profitable business - that, of course, is the only object of the exercise.

Secondly, anyone who obtains a part of his living by displaying wares and/or services before the general public must grasp the fundamental principles essential to successful advertising. Every such person must be competent in both drafting and displaying advertisements. Furthermore, the knack must be required of constantly hitting on both new ideas and methods of presentation.

THAT IS INDISPENSABLE TO ANY SUCCESS - THE CREATION OF NEW IDEAS. Most of us in selling or buying cannot employ an advertising agent; apart from the cost, speed is of the essence. Our goods and services, the demand for them and the competition from rivals are all rapidly changing. Today we must be composing tomorrows` displays. Our very living depends on both the pulling power of those ideas and the speed in which they appear before the public. We do not have the time to brief an advertising agent and to wait for a rough draft.

Thirdly, to manufacture a particular item is easy. Well, it is easy after the machinery has been designed, made and installed in the factory. Once all that is achieved mass production will do the rest. Thereafter, the machinery will produce a vast stock of goods and, here is the rub, it must all be sold. It takes a clever person to keep constantly producing first-class advertisements so that all the goods are sold at a reasonable profit. Unless the advertiser/salesperson sells the stock to buyers in sufficient quantity to keep production running the company, their employees and associates in business will all suffer. You see, the advertiser is essential to the well-being of the business in which he works. That is so important to keep in mind. Those who compose drafts have, to a great extent, commerce in their hands.

From the comments in the last three paragraphs it is clearly seen that advertising is crucial in nearly all aspects of life. The world is highly competitive - rivalry is cut throat - so your displays must rise above the average or sink and not stand out from the visually noisy crowd. You must now take immediate action. It is this - throw away the outdated past and march aggressively into the future with displays that really work and that positively earn both their keep and yours. I know that it is so easy to write those sentiments and so difficult to put them into action in the real hard world. From this point onwards digest and, as appropriate, start putting into practice the ideas given in these pages and become a master in the noble art of composing and displaying money-earning displays.

Let me be audacious and give a warning and see to what extent all those awe-inspiring technological inventions will assist you when preparing drafts. The revolution has, and is, giving a wide range of beneficial aids culminating in the World Wide Web. It is so easy to sit back, relax and believe (hope) that all those phenomenal devices will do your job for you. As stated at the start of the section on salesmanship they are vital aids and save so much time and effort and enable you to have immediate contact with customers, suppliers, competitors, et al. But in the final analysis only your personal effort will produce eye-catching drafts that will really work for you. No device can produce an advertisement or decide in which media it should be displayed. You - and you alone - have to put pen to paper and compose those enticing drafts. Isn't that a sobering thought?

NEVER FORGET THAT YOU MUST DRAFT SUCCESSFUL DISPLAYS THAT STAND OUT FROM THE CROWD AND THEN WORKING WITH ALL YOUR TECHNICAL EQUIPMENT IT WILL BE A WINNING DISPLAY.

8
WHAT IS ADVERTISING?

It is useful to consider advertising as a combative activity. Both advertising and marketing are generally ways to increase the sale of products and services. For that reason both are used to break down a buyer's resistance. That is there sole objective. The negative mood of a potential buyer will either prevent a sale or make it much more difficult and expensive to obtain. Therefore, a display must keep in mind that it is clearly a conflict between the advertiser (the seller) and the reader or listener of that advertisement (the buyer). So, without any doubt, an advertiser must remember that when he composes a draft it is **HIM (on his own) V THEM.** Again, you see, he is on his own.

Although it is not necessary to get bogged down with too much theory some examination of the background to the subject will be useful. As a start it must be realised that advertising is communicating a message to the reader or listener. It is persuasion or, put another way, visual or sonic salesmanship. It is creating the right image and has two main targets.

Firstly, to catch the eye or ear of the reader or listener.

Secondly, to create the essential vital instant impression. That impression must not instantly fade. It must remain with the reader or listener until the message has registered. As an example, with a sales advertisement (discussed hereafter) that will be goods or services actually sold. I call that impression **THE FIRST AND LASTING IMPRESSION.** It must keep nagging at the reader or listener until he is forced - or charmed - into action. Often, of course, an individual will not act for, to him, that display has not been successful. Life tells you that you will not win them all.

It must be clearly understood that advertisements are divided into two distinctive groups although there is a certain amount of overlapping. The two groups comprise (1) sales advertisements - all those displays that endeavour to sell goods or services and (2) publicity advertisements - displays that endeavour to sell a specific name and/or brand of goods or services.

SALES ADVERTISEMENTS

Their aim is to sell specific goods or services from that display. The actual wares are stated in the display. In the main these displays are used by persons whose sole aim is to sell from that advertisement and do not explicitly seek any other publicity. If the wares are sold the display has successfully done its job.

As a simple example, a car owner urgently wants to dispose of his second-hand Mini and advertises in the local paper. He realised that he would have active competition and must draft and display the advertisement without delay. He wants the cash to help pay the monthly mortgage repayments on his house - he is slipping into arrears. A really good display must be composed. A dreary and tired stereotype display would be lost amongst many other similar hastily written ones. With just a little forethought and the glimmer of an idea the display could have great visual impact and truly stand out from its sleepy neighbours. That would be a true sales advertisement. The owner was only interested in selling his Mini; he wasn't interested in publicising his name...purely in selling his car. A true sales advertisement. As an aside - the display stated "a Mini car with mini petrol consumption" and that brief tag sold the car.

Here is a descriptive example of a sales advertisement being composed. The car to be sold is a prestige nearly new BMW car. It is in super condition and possesses all the latest gadgets. Without a shadow of doubt it is a connoisseur's car; one that any car lover would be proud to own. You have decided to use the Motor Car Edition of the local paper and are seeking a heading for a classified display; one which will stand out from the mob.

Your thoughts are working along these lines "...in design and appearance the car is exquisite...in fact, it is a **Beautiful** car...it would be very difficult to find another car - from any maker - in such magnificent condition...that is the second word I seek **Magnificent**. The car has all the latest top grade and exclusive instruments and gadgets. That's the third word I seek **Wonderful** comes quickly to mind." So, there is the heading I seek -

BEAUTIFUL...MAGNIFICENT...WONDERFUL

A good heading? Well, without any doubt it describes the car but might be a little over the top. However, the unusual display will be confirmed when viewers inspect the car; no one will be disappointed. An observation - is the motor car edition of the local paper the right media to advertise a prestige BMW? That question is considered later in this section; in the meantime you consider your views.

Within this group are advertisements that seek to purchase items. That is "wanted advertisements" as opposed to sales ones. The aspiration is the same - drafts must be attract and activate. In this section the expression "sales advertisements" include displays that seek to purchase items.

The prime and only purpose of sales advertisements is to sell a specific item/s and not to **intentionally** publicise the name of the advertiser. Of course, there is always an element of publicity and that is all to the good; the constant advertising campaign of sales advertisements will be beneficial to the advertiser. Even so, it must be clearly understood that the fundamental purpose is to deal with a specific item/s at that point in time. A sale is a be all and end all of the exercise. Do not get confused. When you are drafting any sales advertisement make absolutely sure that the reader's eye goes straight to the main message and is not diverted to a too boldly displayed name of the advertiser. Estate agents are too prone to consider that their names are the most important item in the display. Be that as it may, estate agent's displays are always a combination of sales and publicity. That is **PUBLICITY** being a constant feature of every display carrying the estate agent's name and **SALES** being the properties for sale.

Consider another exception to the rule. When a national or international company is involved and its name is widely known and trusted by the public the name may be as important as the product itself with both immediately registering in the mind of the observer. These advertisements are generally the work of advertising agents.

PUBLICITY ADVERTISEMENTS

This group's aim is to sell a name or a brand of goods. The prime purpose is publicity; it is to brainwash the reader or listener. In the main these displays are used by large firms who deal in mass sales of inexpensive goods or, paradoxically, in limited sales of expensive top of the range prestige goods. True publicity advertisements are expensive and the market being sought must be capable of producing sales to support the cost. Hence, such displays are only economic in limited circumstances and are usually handled by advertising agents. Many are extremely clever and have a tremendous impact on the buying public. To be truly successful this group must be used over a long period of time and to near saturation point. Hence, once planted in the public's mind it cannot be easily erased by a competitor. Think - Oxo-Cadburys-Sotheby and so on. You can learn from these displays. Read and consider the splendid presentations in Country Life and the various County magazines.

The contrast between the displays in the local press and those in the glossy magazines illustrates the basic difference between these two distinctive categories of advertisements. Each serves its own useful purpose and it's pulling power and style is, of necessity, different. A cynic would say that it all boils down to money and it must be admitted that he could be right. Most of the displays in the glossy upmarket magazines come within the combined publicity/sales group although the dominant purpose is generally to publicise the name and purpose of the business. Of course, all advertisements set out to sell goods or services however they are classified.

As already seen there is an overlap between sales and publicity displays. In fact, each classification possesses features from the other grouping but, and this is very important, each must fall squarely into its own group. As an example of this consider that if the car salesman proposing to sell his Mini had been in business as a car salesman his approach would have been different. The advertisement gave publicity to his name and business, a plus being the bonus of an opportunity of selling other cars to persons who noticed his display. Also, to a limited extent it was a sales advertisement for it put before potential buyers the mini which he wished to sell.

Publicity display's hammer the message home. They saturate the public domain until they become (virtually) a part of the English language. That is, of course, an overstatement but it does reinforce the message being given. Publicity displays prove beyond doubt that

Lenin was absolutely right in having as his motto just two simple words - **ceaselessly explain.**

SO, LET`S DEFINE ADVERTISING

Advertising is the first indispensable step to selling goods and services. It forms the basis of all business and trade and, also, of many other aspects of everyday life. Nearly all professions, businesses and trades could not reach anywhere near their real potential without it. The responsibility falling on draftsmen is formidable for, as already stated, unless money-earning displays are drafted and attract profitable business many enterprises would fail or just drift along making a poor living for their owners and their staff.

To understand the true meaning of advertising it is beneficial to research the dictionary definition of "to advertise". Look at a dictionary and you will see these include - to inform, to give notice to, to give notice of, to give public information about merits claimed for, to present or praise, to make publicity, to encourage enterprise, to notify, to offer for sale, et al. Two inherent features of these definitions are visual attraction and the giving of information. That concisely defines advertising - **FIRST CATCH THE EYE, THEN RAM HOME THE MESSAGE.**

Which group of persons are the best advertisers? The answer to that question is both wide ranging and controversial. Without any qualms my personal view is - some estate agents. That is not because I have been an estate agent and have drafted hundreds of displays. Estate agents advertise everywhere, the main media being local and national newspapers, all types of magazines, the internet and their display boards. To a certain extent estate agents have the best of both worlds for the majority of their displays are both sales and publicity ones. It would be beneficial to take a close look at their displays in the local papers and in The Sunday Times and Country Life. You will learn much about how to describe products. Dismiss those that use the words attractive, well-situated, desirable and sought-after. They are the hastily prepared displays of the everyday estate agent. That will be a good lesson to you and you will clearly see how uninviting such descriptions are to the readers. Seek out and concentrate on those that are original in layout and clearly state the features that are likely to motivate a reader to want to inspect the property. Those displays that make you sigh, "I`d love to inspect that property", have been carefully drafted and not thrown together. That is the real purpose of the display - to motivate a reader to want to inspect the property then the salesperson can do his job and, hopefully, a sale can be arranged. That, you see, is the first step in the sales programme in all sales situations. Create a desire and give the salesperson a chance of exercising his skills.

From the last paragraph it is clearly seen that the first step in the sales process is advertising. It is a lesson that you must never forget. When drafting keep constantly before you that the draft must create a desire; when that desire is activated the move towards success is started. The reader must be motivated to action; otherwise the advertiser and the display have failed. This is so important that it is repeated several times in this chapter.

There is no doubt that the finest joint sales/publicity display is the estate agent`s board. Depending on location it will be seen by hundreds of people every day. What a wonderful (virtually) free plug for the agent. Can you think of a better publicity stunt? Try to create a similar type of display for your own purpose. You will not find it easy.

THE OBJECTIVES OF ADVERTISING

There is generally only one objective to advertising and that is to make money. Whether you are buying or selling, whether it is a sales or publicity advertisement, somewhere in the background is the wish to create wealth for the advertiser. Otherwise, why do you advertise? Consider for one moment the apt words of George Orwell, "If you compare commercial advertising with political propaganda, one thing that strikes you is its relative intellectual honesty. The advertiser at least knows what he is aiming at - that is money". You see, the entire world knows your aim. So, do not beat about the bush. Be bold, be impudent and forcefully display your goods or services. Your displays create and attract business which benefit the majority of the population; thus, providing employment and goods for consumption or services for all to use. There is no need to hide the main objective of the exercise. When drafting your aim must be - this display must sell my goods or services, it must motivate the reader. Much better still use positive thinking - this advertisement **WILL** be a success. Do not be shy and hide that real motive. Only if you **REALLY** have faith in your ability will you succeed.

THE OBJECTIVE - TO ADVERTISE AND TO DO PROFITABLE BUSINESS

An advertisement should be thought of as a bridge between buyer and seller, telling the public what is for sale and endeavouring to persuade them to cross the bridge and buy. All displays must be so designed that they tempt prospective customers across **YOUR** bridge and into a discussion with **YOU**. The most successful advertiser is the one who makes it easy for readers. Most traffic will use a bridge that provides a short cut; nearly everyone takes the line of least resistance. Therefore, it is vital that you keep displays as conspicuous, clear-cut and informative as possible. The display must, for instance, clearly state where and when the advertiser can be found and he must be there waiting for calls. It is infuriating trying to contact someone who has given an incorrect or incomplete address and more infuriating to keep ringing a number and getting no reply.

Here is an admirable maxim for draftsmen - the only objective is to get potential customers across that dividing bridge as simply and as quickly as possible. When potential customers are met face-to-face there is the greatest opportunity of striking a deal.

The overriding aim that draftsmen must keep before them is crystallised in just five words – **TO CREATE AND ATTRACT BUSINESS.** Under the umbrella of this dominant objective other vital features of really money-making advertising are considered under the following six headings:

1. ADVERTISING IS PERSUASION AND VISUAL/AUDIL SALESMANSHIP

A salesman can rarely sell without speaking. An advertiser cannot win without being persuasive in a visual or audio sense. Nevertheless, the effect must be politely aggressive. It must shout from the display, "Look, here...see what I`m offering you..." It must be sufficiently conspicuous to attract the eyes or ears away from the many other competing happenings. Those completing elements include other advertisements and all the other items of everyday living within range of the reader's eyes and ears. Your displays have quite a job to do. In spite of that the appeal must be pleasing and in good taste. It must be dignified persuasion and never brash or vulgar boasting. The message should be fed to readers or listeners so that it is not realised that anyone is trying to influence them in any way. All of us like to think that we bought an item because we were clever and hate having to admit that it was sold to us. You must come to understand the significance of that statement which is discussed elsewhere in this book.

Before you read the last paragraph you may well have thought that "brash and vulgar boastings" are, by their very nature the only way to attract attention. That can, of course, be so when selling cheap (and nasty) goods. However, in the main it does pay to use dignified displays for those brash displays will devalue your wares and the overall impression that you are trying so hard to impart. It must be readily admitted that the border line between the brash and the respectable is difficult to both define and to acknowledge when drafting. As you read both published advertisements and the drafts that you are producing you will soon realise where to draw the line. Experience is a great teacher and the difference between the right and wrong way will very soon become apparent. As an example, a trader selling vegetables in an open market must use his voice to tell passers-by the excellent value being offered. That style of "brash and vulgar boastings" is acceptable in those conditions.

2. ADVERTISING IS BEING CLEAR ABOUT PRIORITIES

Quite simply this means drafting to clearly illustrate the goods or services on offer. The priority is to sell, not to show the world how clever you are. That will become obvious when real money-earning sales are produced. Do not get carried away by being verbose. Keep the message brief and simple. This point is illustrated by the old display - Johnnie Walker never stands still. There were no wasted words. Just five words and the story was well told. Super.

3. ADVERTISING IS CREATING THE RIGHT IMPRESSION

A suggestion - an idea or a mere thought is implanted in the reader's mind. It must unconsciously keep nagging away until he is forced into some action. A mere first impression is inadequate. A "first and lasting impression" has to be made. That means that the reader becomes a customer, if not, all the effort has been wasted. To repeat, to ram the message home a display has two functions - **Firstly, to catch the eye or ears and, secondly, to create an impression/desire that lasts until its objective has been achieved.** It may be considered monotonous to keep coming back to that last sentiment but it must be vigorously impressed to all those who draft or intend to draft displays - and want to be truly successful.

When considering this heading it will be realised that to create an impression the display **MUST STAND OUT FROM THE CROWD.** Those last six words (which stand out from the crowd!) will often appear elsewhere in this section. Their importance is such that repetition is imperative. Remember that all the time your displays are competing with others. There is no way whatsoever that you can throw off that annoying liability. It will not go away. It must be tackled head on by right thinking and by constant learning as you plan and compose your drafts.

Consider and use this idea - ask your colleagues, friends, family, et al. to give their honest opinion on your ideas, drafts and completed advertisements. Ask, "Does this draft impress you, is it boring, is it really bold enough? Learn from their criticism and do not be too proud to thank them for their help.

The draftsman must use constantly changing tactics. Rewarding drafts like the Johnnie Walker cannot be copied. It is too easy - and not profitable - to copy and slightly alter another advertiser's draft. To do so is just not good enough. To a certain extent we are all somewhat lazy but laziness, like most disadvantages, can be cured. New ideas and different concepts must be continuously investigated and suitable concepts used in your work. Thinking and scheming is somewhat like perpetual motion for as you use your mind it will, with experience, produce a never ending string of new suggestions and new slants on older material. The creation and use of ideas is dealt with in chapter fifteen.

You can be assured that once you get on the right track and put together some business producing ideas you will want to push further forward and never look back at yesterday's old ideas. In fact, you will be far too busy and elated to even think about it.

I am, of course, an avid reader of all types of estate agent's advertisements. It is surprising that many agents advertise a property for two or three weeks with exactly the same wording. Obviously the property was not sold from the first display - it was not a success. So, why waste time and money repeating a failure. A few minutes thinking about a new idea and wording or a complete new angle could change a failure to success. To steal a much used phrase, it is not rocket science; it is just plain common commercial sense.

4. GOOD DRAFTS KEEP THE ADVERTISER AHEAD OF ALL COMPETITORS

How do you know that your displays are keeping you ahead of competitors? In that respect you must tread very carefully. Consider the following two comments:

Firstly, the profit and loss account is a great barometer and it rarely gives a false reading. Rising profits are one sign that advertising is working. However, that could be a false assumption. Another unrelated factor may be helping to push profits along. Taking the business overall it probably does not matter which component is responsible for generating profits. But, beware. Say, for example, you have a virtual monopoly and there is no competing newsagent within a three mile radius. Right out of the blue a competitor opens just around the corner from your shop. Your profits start to suffer. The reason for your old profit growth has gone; competition has arrived. If you had operated a sensible advertising policy including handbills to all properties in local roads the competitor's research may have resulted in him being scared off by your enterprise or, having opened, found it virtually impossible to encroach on your well-secured business. The lesson is this - even when all is going well keep drafting eye-catching displays and do remember that no one owes you a living. Do not tempt fate by relaxing.

Secondly, in this example you are already drafting and using first-class displays. You are not relaxing and sales are healthy and rising. Week after week you spent much valuable time on drafting. Unlike the last example there is no new competitor around the corner. Even so you do not rest on your laurels. In any business or sales exercise to relax is only a step away from seeing profits wilt. The answer is to keep exploring for new ideas. Although it takes much research, hard slog and the constant use of brain power to continually produce acceptable drafts it must be done. The main restraint is time. The solution is to set aside a period each week or each month - it depends on the timing and extent of your advertising - in which to undertake this essential task. If you do not make this sacrifice your drafts will begin to look tired. The reason for that falling away is that you are attempting to draft in between doing other tasks, you are not fully concentrating on one job in hand and are becoming a little slapdash. You will not be the competitor that all rival's fear. So, **NOW** enter that selected research time in your diary and do not let any event or individual interrupt you. I considered my ideas and suitable drafts for advertising at home every Thursday evening. It was a nice quiet time away from everyday work.

Never forget that time spent on considering advertisement and publicity generally is never wasted. Of course, it is even more beneficial if that time is taken outside of profitable business time.

5. ADVERTISING MUST BE AIMED AT A CLEARLY DEFINED MARKET

Experienced traders will know the right way to attract potential customers but demand is an ever-changing fashion and no reliance can be placed on (even) yesterday's methods or results. Although laymen may consider that a firm wishing to sell goods and services has the entire population as potential buyers that is rarely so. At any given point in time a trader's wares will only be of interest to a small fraction of the community and, more to the point, in fierce competition with many similar wares which are being aggressively advertised.

As an example of a clearly defined and very restricted market a top-flight jeweller would not advertise exquisite and expensive jewellery in the local press. Readers of that media would not have the wealth to buy his wares. The vehicle for display would, for example, be glossy magazines for it would be known from both experience and repute that such media would be read by the affluent few - his most likely customers. Furthermore, the actual displays would be of persons and articles associated with luxury living. He might select the picture of a beautiful and expensively dressed lady - obviously a duchess or a star footballer's wife, stepping daintily into her shining Rolls Royce or, maybe, entering her magnificent country mansion. Many other likely scenes of such opulence come readily to mind. The draftsman might consider that a more acceptable image would be a well-known pop star boarding his helicopter. It would depend so much on the market that the advertiser sought to reach.

Nearly all readers of glossy magazines associate themselves with million-pound living and with the opulent jewellery and similar expensive items being advertised. That is motivation by association. Well-heeled wealthy readers will subconsciously muse...such style, such elegance. I must visit that jeweller...that really is me.

Conversely, a person wanting to sell an inexpensive terraced two-bedroomed house in the shabby back street of a provincial town is unlikely to use a quality Sunday newspaper. Readers of those papers would be unlikely customers for such a house in that type of area. Again, the display would not be aimed at the right market. The correct media would be the local press.

A skilled advertiser knows how to find and harry the right media. I am a reader of all types of advertisements and time and time again the rule is broken. Time, effort and money are wasted. The overall result is lost business and lost goodwill. The unsuitable/wrong media will only profit the owners of those media used.

The inexperienced advertiser must ascertain the right market before putting pen to paper. It is likely that the result obtained by a poor drafted display in the **RIGHT** media will better a superbly thought-out and drafted display in the **WRONG** media. That illustrates that all that valuable time devoted to seeking the right media was time well spent. At least in the right media your display will be read by persons likely to be potential customers.

6. THE IMPRESSION CREATED BY ADVERTISING DOES NOT STOP WHEN THE DISPLAY IS OVER

The impact of advertising is not restricted to only persuading a person to purchase or sell although that is the essential aspiration.

With sales advertisements it goes without saying that wrongly displayed and/or badly worded advertisements do not sell as many wares as perfectly placed and well - worded ones. Nevertheless, a word of warning is needed. All those bad and indifferent displays have the additional drawback of giving the impression of a poorly run business and that reflects on the advertiser. It is likely to harm his short and long term prospects. It will be readily seen that not looking after your displays could bring a host of serious problems resulting in a reduction in sales and bad publicity generally. A double whamming. Never forget that bad and/or sloppy displays will be noticed by potential customers who could be lost as real money-spending ones. They will avoid a ramshackled looking business like the plague.

With publicity advertisements the damage done by using inferior drafts can be severe. The very device that should be radiating benefits is failing and, thus, producing the opposite impact. It should be realised that it is far easier to create a bad impression than a good one. What a waste of all your resources. Furthermore, the more damaging the impact the longer it will remain in the reader's mind. It is often said that any publicity is good publicity, but that is only true to a limited extent. Bad publicity frightens away potential customers and that cannot in any circumstances whatsoever be beneficial. A bad advertisement is a bad advertisement - there is no argument there.

You will read many times in this book that your success or lack of it depends entirely on **YOU** - you will receive very little help from anyone else when the chips are down. It is just not possible to pass the blame to anyone else. It is vital to always keep well in mind that it all depends on **YOU.**

REMEMBER THAT FIRST-CLASS DRAFTING IS...

* PERSUASION AND VISUAL/AUDILE SLAESMANSHIP

* BEING CLEAR ABOUT PRIORITIES

* CREATING THE RIGHT IMPRESSION

* KEEPING AHEAD OF COMPETITORS

* AIMING AT CLEARLY DEFINED MARKETS

* THE IMPRESSION DOES NOT STOP AFTER A SALE

IT IS VITAL TO SUCCESS THAT YOU KEEP AT THE FOREMOST OF YOUR THOUGHTS THAT NOTHING HAPPENS UNLESS YOU MAKE IT

A WORD OF WARNING

Having reached this stage in the book and digested the above summary you may well be reaching the conclusion that you may never be able to think-up/create lucrative advertisements. It is all too much. If that is your reaction you are entirely mistaken. Look at your situation in the following manner. You purchased this book and have read to this page - that must demonstrate that you want to become a good draftsman. So, keep reading and do not throw in the towel. What you learn from lessons in this book plus that practical experience gained whilst working in the commercial world will soon produce well-worded and eye-catching displays. As in all things there is no easy road to success. It has to be earned. To quit now would be throwing away all you have learned to date and that will get you nowhere. Do not take my word for it, keep pushing on and you will soon rejoice that the advice given in this paragraph truly helped you along the way.

9
SELECTING AND USING THE MEDIA

The selection of the right media is without any shadow of doubt the most important aspect considered as you are putting together an advertising campaign. This is so whether one single or many insertions are to be undertaken. As already stated a well-drafted and nicely displayed advertisement in the wrong media is a complete waste of resources. To take two extreme examples, it would be laughable to advertise a magnificent and expensive tiara in the local paper or a low priced terraced house in the poorer part of a town on TV. It may well sell the house but at what cost? It is seen from those examples that the correct media has to be carefully selected in order to be both economic and to reach the desired audience.

Even the most meticulously planned publicity campaign will only succeed when it is expertly turned into a decent eye-catching display of both words and, where applicable, pictures and the message conveyed to the appropriate audience. In a bid to reach that goal the first question is - where and when shall I advertise? That is the sixty-four thousand dollar question and in itself poses more questions. The question that sums-up the search for the right media is this - where am I likely to find the highest number of potential customers at an economic price? It is as simple as that!

The search for the right media is actually a search to find the right newspaper or other media which attracts the most potential customers that you seek. As an example, a top-flight West End jeweller of repute who is accustomed to dealing with high society - duchesses, lords, pop stars et al, will know from experience that his customers read glossy magazines such as Country Life, The Tatler, The Field and so on. He need look no further for his buyers. Imagine the state of the profit and loss account if he advertised in the local press of a small town. Likewise, by using research, experience and everyday observations all potential advertisers will discover which media will produce real potential customers.

There is an interesting range of media. In fact, a most confusing range. Do not forget that they are advertising for your business. Listen to what they say...then, make your own decision. You may find that you can "do a deal" with an advertising manager for he, like you, is seeking business. He will be very willing to discuss your plans for an advertising campaign.

The question to keep to the fore is this - is the average reader or listener of your display likely to be able to afford the wares you are about to advertise. If the answer is "yes" consider the second question - are those readers or listeners likely to want my goods? Taken together those two questions will be of great benefit as you decide on a media.

Within the media there is a wide range of expenditure ranging from the least expensive in the local press and the free newspapers to the very expensive on the national TV screens and on the Internet. It must be borne in mind that to be really effective advertising costs must be looked at in relation to both the value and the quantity of the items being advertised. This is evident when viewing any car manufacturers` displays on the TV screen. The overall expenditure will be considerable as there are many complicated artistic and technical stages from the concept of the idea right through to the appearance of the completed display on the TV screen. Even so, that expenditure will be worked into the overall budget of the firm. It will be an acceptable proportion of the overall cost when the cars produced are sold at economic prices. The total advertising costs divided by the number of cars produced and sold will look realistic and will (probably) prove that advertising pays. Of course, the manufacturers` calculations will not be as simple as that but that is the theory of costing whether or not advertising pays.

It is interesting to observe that although a truly successful advertisement campaign is generally necessary to produce a viable and profitable overall business, the reverse is, also, true. That is, unless the items being produced are well-made, up-to-date and competitively marketed even the best advertising campaign is likely to fail. An advertising campaign is part and parcel of the overall running costs of a business and cannot be relied upon to save a badly run organisation producing inferior goods at the wrong price. Of course, poor over-priced goods may sell but you do not want to be the person who displays or sells such wares. There is no future in that activity although, as an aside, Aneurin Bevan said, "If you are selling shoddy goods you have to be a good salesman". True, but that is not a course to be pursued.

It will be realised from the last paragraph that advertising must not be isolated from the overall business. The advertising department of all businesses, whether it is a single person in a small firm or a separate department of a large concern, must work as an integral part of the overall business. The person/s responsible for advertising/publicity will know all the "ins and outs" of the market in which he operates. It is essential that his views, particularly on pricing, are passed back to those whose job it is to run the company. It is futile, a great waste of resources, when the advertising department are trying to market and sell virtually unsaleable wares. An exchange of views is the life blood of a profitable concern. This paragraph teaches a vital lesson and illustrates the true value that a responsible and experienced drafter is to the company. Additionally, it emphasises that when an advertisement is drafted the drafter **MUST** have knowledge of the subject matter being sold otherwise his drafted displays will not do the job. A few words to remember – the successful draftsman is just like a competent salesman, a person with the gift of the (written) gab.

It must be remembered that it is not only the total cost of a display that is important. It is the benefits that are likely to flow from that expenditure that proves whether it is money well spent or wasted. A car manufacturer knows the volume of cars being manufactured over a given period and the number that must be economically sold. Those glossy publicity displays not only publicise the name of the firm and the goods on offer but are, also, of inestimable value as they are indirectly publicising the showrooms, garages and the like that have the vital front line job of selling that manufacturer's cars. Whatever way the displays are worded the ultimate objective is to help salespersons sell at the point of sale. Those "on the spot concerns" do their own local advertising in the local press, the County magazines and the like. So, it will be realised that publicity and sales advertisements merge with one common objective - to sell cars to the public. At that point, the prosperity of the manufacturing company is determined. Again this proves that drafters of both types of advertisements have, to a great extent, the prosperity of their companies in their hands. That is further proof that if you produce first-class drafts **THAT SELL** you will be sought-after and never unemployed. To help you reach that happy state is the purpose of this section of this book. Although this paragraph refers to cars being advertised the same principles apply to all other goods and services.

Let us move to the other extremity of the business world. As an example, a small business selling second-hand furniture from a poorish secondary shopping position in small towns is unlikely to be able to afford expensive publicity. In any event it would not be economic; it would be a waste of money and effort. However, the trader must advertise. The name over the shop would be a direct advertisement although only to passers-by. More potential customers must be attracted to the business. The answer is that low cost displays in the local press and in free newspapers are likely to be read by persons who want to buy or sell reasonably priced furniture locally. Despite being low cost two purposes will be achieved. Firstly, to sell furniture in the shop and awaiting purchasers is the main purpose; to buy furniture. That is to attract retail trade. Secondly, to bring and keep the name of the trader and his business before the public. It will then, over a period of time, become known that a local shop trades in second-hand furniture. The trader may not be aware of the last function. A wise trader would realise that there is always tomorrow and would be content to sell a steady flow of items and to know that within the town a growing number of persons are aware of the existence of his business. That example illustrates that a simple low cost sales display also acts as a publicity one albeit to a limited extent. It is repeated again, the reason why all displays must be well-drafted is that the image created will reflect on the advertiser and his business generally. It is a tough energy and money consuming task building-up goodwill; but keep in mind that it can be lost in a flash.

It has been seen that there is a wide range of media available and, as a general rule, publicity advertisers are able to spend considerably more than sales ones. With a successful campaign more revenue is produced and the image should remain with the reader for a long period of time; often with a truly national campaign the message is (almost) everlasting.

At first sight it seems that there is a really wide and varied selection of media at the advertiser's command. However, this range is narrowed by the rule that displays must only appear where they are likely to attract the maximum potential customers. Bearing that in mind the advertiser nearly always becomes somewhat restricted in choice. The most frequent media come within these headings:

A The Internet - the information superhighway. See hereafter. This includes mobile 'phone advertising.

B Television - coverage being local, national or international. Television advertising is expensive and is generally used by large companies for both sales and publicity displays. Its wide influence is of particular appeal to national companies who wish to get and keep their names and produces before a wide range of viewers. It is important to remember that a TV advertisement must be seen when it appears; one minute it is on screen and virtually gone in a flash. Whereas, for example, a newspaper display is in being to be read until the paper is destroyed; although with sales advertisements its main use is only whilst the contents of the display is current. Also, it is easier to obtain addresses, telephone numbers and so on. Whereas that information is harder to see and record when flashed onto the TV screen. This brief comment illustrates the difference in operation between TV and other types of advertisements.

C Daily and evening newspapers - coverage being local, national and international. For those businesses that mainly rely on local trade the local and free newspapers are extremely useful.

D Week-end newspapers, particularly The Sundays

with wide national coverage. These deserve a separate heading as for certain types of businesses and professions they have a wide and strong pulling power. As an example, The Sunday Times is particularly strong in the property world especially in the medium/higher price range of properties for sale.

E Weekly newspapers - including the extremely useful and popular county and town editions.

F Prestige glossy monthly magazines - coverage being local (county towns and similar), national and international. All these are splendid vehicles for advertising luxury fashions, jewellery, watches, cars, et al. and are read by the more affluent persons in society. There are many attractive and extremely well-run town/county magazines that give a wide local coverage.

G Monthly and weekly magazines - not within group F - including those featuring world affairs, national politics, hobbies, business, general and learned societies, et al. and with tremendous pulling powers in their respective expertise. There is a very wide selection of titles within this group.

H Trade and business magazines and journals published by professional, business and learned organisations.

I Radio Broadcasting. There is an increasing array of local - some very local - stations. Hence, of real interest to very local advertising.

In addition to the above media there are many useful advertising methods which may be grouped as follows:

Posters displayed in many different types of locations.

Business, trade and other exhibitions. Also, many

charity organisations whose programmes for various functions give good scope for concentrated local publicity. Exhibitions can range from a local one in the Town Hall to a national event at Olympia. A worthwhile cause.

Programmes - theatre, cinema, sports events, local charity events, Bank holiday shows in local parks, et al. Also useful are displays in year books, various guides and local directories. A wide range from displays on local maps to the ever useful Yellow Pages.

Miscellaneous hand bills with a wide variety of methods of distribution, displays on the side of taxis and `buses. Objects of various descriptions given away for publicity purposes - key labels, car key rings, pencils, pens, penknives, blotters, diaries, calendars and car stickers are but a few items that can be stamped with business names and publicity slogans.

The groupings above summarise certain methods available but it must be borne in mind that it is only a general guide and is not an exhaustive list. It will help you to conjure up your own ideas which, hopefully, have not previously been used. Individual professions, businesses and trades have their own brand of publicity which can conveniently be termed "custom advertising". Typical examples are estate agents and their boards and oil companies who display banner announcements at motor racing meetings.

Some dramatic advertising is legally banned or tightly controlled. These include sky writing, sky shouting and offshore radio advertising. Furthermore, in the UK outdoor displays are under the strict control of the planning regulations. If in any doubt do take legal advice before expending money on any doubtful undertaking. Never in any circumstances run the risk of advertising illegally. That will, in itself, be a bad advertisement for the advertiser.

THE INTERNET
THE WORLDWIDE WEB

The importance of the Internet cannot be over-estimated. In fact, nowadays it is now rare for a business not to be connected thereto. It would take a complete book to explain and discuss its uses and great benefits. In the context of advertising it is sufficient to state that it is having a devastating impact on both commerce and everyday life. This means that instant communication has become one of the fastest growing media. You will, of course, find it both necessary and desirable to use the WWW to reach your clients and customers. You will, however, find that it pays to employ an advertising agency to help you when advertising on the WWW.

HOW DO YOU FIND AND CONTACT THE CORRECT MEDIA?

Look no further than the Internet which provides information on all matters under the sun. Remember that if needs be the Internet may be used in some cafes and in most reference libraries. Other than those sources reference libraries have directories relating to most professions, businesses and trades. For local knowledge there are no better places than the publicity departments in most town halls and local tourist offices. A call at the offices of the local newspaper will help you to mass much information about their paper/s and the surrounding area. They will also help you to compose displays for their own paper/s!

A most valuable aid to your selection of media is Willing's Press Guide - for details of this essential reading see the Internet or ask to see a copy at your local library. There are Guides for the UK, Europe and the World.

There is no need to consider separately each media group. That would not be time well spent. The basic principles expounded in these pages are applicable to each individual group. The advertiser, like a salesperson/negotiator, must put those principles into practice in his own individual manner. The lessons set out in this section and the ideas that you will formulate must be taken from the academic world into the rough, tough and real world of commerce. Again, it must be emphasised that in the final analysis it all depends on **YOU.** Only you, after due consideration, can choose the correct media for your displays.

Within each individual media there is a range of alternatives. As an example, having decided that newspapers are suitable the next question is - what coverage is required? Is it local, regional or national? There is a choice from a staggering array of newspapers. As already stated Willing's Press Guide is a super source of information and a glance through its pages will be rewarding. It could be detrimental to the success of a campaign to select the wrong alternative as it would be to choose the wrong media. So, the advertiser's skill is to select both the right media and the right alternative. At any crossroad or road junction there is normally only one correct road to be taken, the road map must be closely studied. An advertiser will only select both the right media and the right alternative by correctly answering the following two questions:

FIRSTLY, WHAT COVERAGE AM I SEEKING?

Coverage is the extent of the geographical influence of each individual display. Thought must be given to the size and scope of the advertiser's business and to the wares being offered. Those considerations must be balanced against the cost of the displays.

A small local firm may only have the capacity to cope with a limited amount of orders and if these are obtained locally a useful saving in package and transport costs will results. There will no need to advertise outside the local area.

A large firm may need regional and/or national coverage to attract enough business to keep its labour force fully employed and to benefit from its size. A chain of local/regional shops may standardise its displays so that each individual shop benefits from all the overall advertising campaigns. A national multiple group would cover an even larger area and standardise to cope for national advertising. It will be realised that in all cases there is an element of local advertising, each individual shop will benefit from all the displays in its immediate catchment area.

As far as the actual wares being sold are concerned the more expensive and/or exceptional they are the wider the coverage required. For example, a person wishes to sell a valuable cubist painting by Braque. The correct coverage would be international. The painting could, for example, be sold in Brighton but unless the owner was extremely lucky not at anywhere near the highest price. There would not be the necessary maximum competition and only extensive national and international competition would take the price realised to its maximum. That example pinpoints why antique dealers do so well; purchases are made locally and sold internationally where competition pushes prices to their maximum.

SECONDLY, WHAT MARKET AM I SEEKING WITHIN THAT COVERAGE?

Having selected the correct coverage the draftsman must then decide what market is being sought. He must ask himself the best and most economic manner in which to reach potential customers. That is the aim always being sought when advertising.

As an example, a single shop retailer dealing in garden accessories requires local coverage which would be read by the greater number of local persons. The display would appear under the appropriate classified heading in the local press and, therefore, be read by potential customers seeking garden accessories. If a local or county newspaper covered areas with houses with gardens - as opposed to town houses with patios or tiny gardens - that would be the newspaper to concentrate on. The search for a potential market has been narrowed. Another method of advertising that the retailer might use could be the distribution of handbills delivered to all areas of the town with properties with gardens. Those selected householders could be potential customer but the percentage who actually buys is likely to be less than from a classified display. The distribution of handbills is a little hit or miss. Returning to the local displays it is right to assume that those readers who take the trouble to seek out and read the classified displays featuring garden accessories are likely buyers. The advertiser has correctly set up his stall to attract the maximum number of potential purchasers. That applies to all professions, businesses and trades - make it as easy as possible for potential customers to see or hear your displays and as easy for those wanting to do business to find you.

The following four illustrations demonstrate the process of selecting media:

1. **ADVERTISER:** Private person, an ordinary man in the street. **GOODS:** Second-hand Ford car of low value. **OBJECTIVE:** To sell the car as quickly as possible with as little expense as possible. **SUGGESTED MEDIA:** Classified display in the local press on the day that cars are specially featured. A display card in a local shop window; low cost but slim chance of success. **COMMENT:** Do not forget the free newspapers that will give a reasonable local coverage.

2. **ADVERTISER:** Private person. **GOODS:** A specialist car. An expensive low mileage Aston Martin. **OBJECTIVE:** To sell the car as soon as possible at a realistic price. Expense not a limiting factor as in example (1). **SUGGESTED MEDIA:** A quality Sunday newspaper, a specialist motor magazine and/or a display on the Internet. **COMMENT:** Purely a sales display, media selected read by wealthy persons who appreciate quality cars. Highlight "prestige" and "luxury". A wider market is being sought than in example (1).

3. **ADVERTISER:** A firm buying and selling cars with commodious showrooms in a prosperous market town. **GOODS:** Many different types of cars at all prices across the spectrum. **OBJECTIVE:** To sell cars. To draw attention to the fact that all types of cars are sold and purchased. To publicise the firm`s business name and its business generally. **SUGGESTED MEDIA:** Local and regional newspapers and motor magazines. Local radio. A web page on the Internet. As top of the range cars handled an occasional display in a glossy county magazine - might be thought that a monthly display was desirable. Consider an occasional regional TV display. Suggestion - consider a discussion with advertising agent. **COMMENT:** All displays will be both sales and publicity ones. The aim is to both sell and buy cars and to give constant publicity to the firm`s name and its numerous products. The firm`s name and business should stay in the reader`s memory until he wants to buy and/or sell a car. The firm should be able to afford to advertise widely as turnover of large stock should give scope for healthy profits. The main basis difference between this firm and (1) and (2) is that potential customers have a wide range of cars from which to choose.

4. ADVERTISER: Specialist firm of car manufacturers. **GOODS:** Their own prestige luxury cars. Extremely expensive. Produced in limited numbers and sold through a limited number of specially selected retailers to whom franchises are granted. No direct selling to the public. **OBJECTIVE:** To keep the firm's name and the quality of their cars before the public and to link the car with opulence. **SUGGESTED MEDIA:** Prestige County magazines. An occasional display on the Internet. Local TV to cover the area where franchise sellers have sway. **COMMENT:** The sole purpose is to help the franchise dealers by back-up displays which would appear less frequently than in (3). Displays just to remind the really wealthy few that these cars exist. A franchise dealer would advertise in the area covered by their own business.

Local radio, regional and national TV and the Internet are important mass media with certainly the greatest impact. What more could an advertiser seek than such an extensive captive audience? Because of this these media are, to varying degrees, expensive and specialist treatment is desired and, thus, are best dealt with by advertising agents. However, the advertiser must not lose sight of the fact that it is his money being spent and his business that is on the line. The advertising agent must be guided as only the advertiser knows the true value and market for his goods or services.

In many countries very large private enterprises sponsor entire radio and/or TV shows and even run news programmes. The story is told of a Latin American TV announcer excitingly exclaiming, "We have just received news of a calamity of such proportions that it dwarfs all disasters of the past. We will be going over to our news room, but first a few words from our sponsors". What a splendid illustration of how to attract and hold attention - if somewhat macabre.

Local advertisers must not forget the free newspapers that are a feature of many towns. They are ideal for selling everyday items and a good vehicle for publicity advertisements for local businesses. Insertions in these papers are realistic in price. These free newspapers were delivered to all properties in the town but that excellent mass publicity is now dying out.

To sum up - when a trader is deciding how to reach the

maximum number of potential purchasers he must cogitate very carefully (1) what area of coverage does he consider is essential and (2) at what market is he aiming within that coverage? Do not forget to ask and answer those two vital questions.

COST EFFICIENCY

Just for one moment imagine that business is falling off and you surmise that the only way to keep your head above water is to immediately slash costs. That is fair enough; it is prudent to be ahead of events. But, and here is the rub, do make sure that any cuts do not have a further debilitating effect on profitability. That is easier said than done. In your worried and somewhat panicky state you do not stop to consider the true havoc that illogical cuts are likely to cause. You seek easy targets. You dismiss the idea of dismissing staff (you are a bit soft - and there are redundancy payments to consider), cutting the rent (your lease fixes that outgoing), your own personal expenses such as those (very) expensive taxi rides (well...maybe...we will consider that at a later date), the monthly bill to The Weekly Herald...ah, that`s it. To cut advertising costs will not hurt anybody. An easy target. You have forgotten potential customers. You ponder...by how much shall I cut that bill? Stop! You have arrived at the wrong question. The correct question is - how can I make my advertising more cost efficient and be a greater attraction to readers?

Your business - or, job if you are an employed salesperson - could be heading for a crisis and your only aim must be to attract more money spending customers. Cutting displays is more than likely to have the reverse effect. On the credit side it will save a little money; on the debit side it is likely to lose valuable new business. So, to summarise, you have now arrived at the right question and have to find the answers that will help you solve your dilemma. Consider the future under the following four headings:

1. ARE YOU USING THE RIGHT MEDIA?

That is an obvious question. It is desirable to look very closely at the media being used and to immediately cancel any that you find are unprofitable. Is the money being spent bringing in sufficient sales to warrant that expenditure? Maybe, expensive and under productive advertising must be reduced or eliminated. Look at other sources in the same media - can you find a less expensive slot? As times generally are hard can you do a deal with the Advertising Manager of the local press on the basis that you will advertise for a set number of weeks at an agreed price? He must be struggling, so a deal may help you both. That angle must be pursued.

Never leave a hole in the advertising budget. If you use a cheaper media only after its use will it be known whether or not it has been a success. Do remember that every change in a marketing programme is very much a trial and error occasion. That is not a reason for doing nothing. It is a reason for directing all your efforts into the right channels. You have a troublesome problem and a solution must be found.

If a competitor seems to be doing well you may consider stealing his thunder. Does he use a different media, advertise on a different day, have a better or different style of advertising and so on? If so, it might be worth giving it a trial run. Do bear in mind this word of warning - the grass always looks (very) much greener away from home, particularly if your own grass is wilting. The competitor may not be as successful as it appears. In any event, it could be that your line of business is in the doldrums. So, for various reasons, look very closely at a competitor who **SEEMS** to be doing more business than you.

2. HAVE YOUR ADVERTISEMENTS BECOME OUTDATED, DULL OR JUST PAST THEIR SELL-BY DATE?

You may have become so used to your own existing publicity that it seems like a very old friend - reliable and safe. If profits show that business is being lost look at your existing advertising programme; not just a glance, take a very detailed close look. Compare it to your competitors' displays. Be brutally honest - you will not upset anyone except yourself. Maybe, that old reliable friend is letting you down.

If the conclusion is that your displays are not up to an excellent standard cutting the budget is not the correct action to take. There is only one way ahead. It is this - you must modernise and bring your style and wording out of the past and into today's world. You have been lost in yesterday's ways and to outsiders - and it is those who matter - you look like an old-fashioned struggling trader...and that, to be honest with yourself...is what you have become. Only immediate and drastic action will save you.

Examine, and if deemed desirable, redesign all aspects of your publicity that you consider are letting you down. Look closely at the media being used, the days on which your displays appear, the design and wording on handbills, if you have an emblem or motto is it out of fashion?...and so on. Throw out all the tired ideas created with such enthusiasm yesterday; they have done their job. After all that sad work has been completed the hard slog begins.

The chapter On Drafting Advertisements will be of considerable help to you. Do remember, do not funk the issue. Take as much time as needed to reassess the way forward; that will not be time wasted. It will be time invested in a more stable and profitable future.

3. ARE YOU PENETRATING THE TARGET MARKET?

This means that you know the market at which your displays are targeted but is that market really being reached and infiltrated? Are you really aiming at the bull's eye? More to the point, are you hitting it? A simple example, you know that the local press is read by persons likely to buy goods or services. That is fine - even if a common fact. But do your displays appear under the correct classification? Should your displays be bolder? A little extra expense and more potential purchasers may notice it. Would a change of days help? Are there any reasons why your potential customers are more likely to read The Daily Post one day rather than another? Is there a local market that makes one day in the week a real "business day"? Do you get the idea? You may well have the right media but that is only half the battle. To win that battle you must hit the right spot at the right time and get the maximum benefit.

An important observation - you will no doubt have realised that answering those four questions will take time and effort. As previously stated the task of getting the business back on track is vital. Do you want to struggle on hoping that something will turn up? It rarely does - unless **YOU** make it happen. So, again it is stated - the way to success is in **YOUR** hands.

4. ARE YOU MAKING THE BEST USE OF RESULTANT ENQUIRIES?

Thereby hangs a rather knotty problem. If you personally take calls it is up to you to give a good service and advice and to close as many deals as possible. That will be fine in a small business where one or two persons look after advertisements and sell therefrom. Consider the more somewhat complex cases where the advertising department of a medium size or large firm are in no way involved with callers and the actual sales process. Of course, the position is the same where a telephonist answers calls; one who has no idea or interest in the profitability of the business. In those cases the person/s who drafts the displays has no involvement with callers or sales. You will realise that the finest and best advertisements in the world do not actually (physically) sell goods or services. They **ATTRACT** potential customers and the vital task of speaking and selling to them is dealt with by another human being and that is where the actual selling comes to the fore. You see, those who compose drafts may well be badly let down by the sales department. Many a churlish, unhelpful, inexperienced or tired salesperson has lost vital business. Then, what should have been a profitable sale campaign turns into an average or poor one. As previously stated it follows that the person in charge of advertising - the drafter - must keep in touch with the sales personnel and get to know the number of callers to a display and, of more value, the number of firm (real) orders that have been achieved. Also, appropriate comments made by callers may be helpful to the drafter. Then, it will soon be sensed if there is a problem on the sales side or that the goods or services on offer are not up to the display`s claims.

If there is a problem the advertising department must be strong and ascertain exactly what is happening. If sufficient potential customers are answering the drafts and, yet, firm sales are poor problems may exist. Firstly, the wares are not seen as good value by callers. That is a problem to be rectified by the management. Secondly, the callers may not be correctly treated by the sales staff and are put off buying. Again, that is a problem to be rectified by the management. It is part of the advertising department's job to ascertain why callers are not being converted into customers and to keep the management so advised.

The advertising department should, by highlighting any reason know to them, realise why business is poor, and keep in touch with those persons who actually speak to callers. Then, the drafters will be able to pinpoint good methods of advertising and to concentrate thereon. In that respect all departments of a firm help each other and that makes a stronger and more focused advertising department. Of course, this exchange of views may from time-to-time prove that the problem is with the advertisements being displayed!

10
ADVERTISING ON THE TELEPHONE

This chapter incorporates the two disciplines of this book rolled into one **SELLING AND ADVERTISING** on the telephone. Even if you do not sell on the telephone you will learn a lot from this chapter.

Nowadays this is an acceptable and a growing way of selling and advertising. But, even so, there are many rogue callers and you must be very careful when getting cold calls. Telephone advertising is divided into two sections. Firstly, cold calls where the caller has no connection with the receiver and is endeavouring to sell wares. This caller must be very careful how he operates as many receivers hate cold calls and slam the `phone down.  Secondly, those callers who are contacting valued customers and are making goodwill calls. It must be remembered that all persons who sell on the `phone are advertising the business represented and themselves.

It seems that most days someone telephones and tries to sell me something. A curse to me but, no doubt, a blessing to the caller when he strikes gold and makes a sale. I have to admit that most callers put me off whilst their first sentence is being spoken. The annoying introductions are, "Your postcode has come up..." - so what, some ones must and "I`m not going to try to sell you anything..." - then, why call?

Many preliminary negotiations take place over the telephone and some deals are concluded without a face-to-face meeting. Numerous companies selling a wide range of goods and services use the telephone to both interest and persuade the receiver to take the next step towards a purchase of their goods. For example, the selling of double glazing, PVC replacement windows, fitted kitchens and bathrooms et al, are often commenced by a telephone a call - a cold call. That is the most difficult exercise for any person to undertake. The aim is to coax the listener to an exhibition, to persuade him to arrange an appointment for a representative to call and so on. It is a way of getting the selling process started. The call is the first contact with a potential customer. It is vital to raise an interest in the first few moments otherwise the caller will hear, "Not today, thank you" and the telephone banged down. The listener is likely to have heard the caller`s name and/or the name of his firm. That is a bad advertisement and the listener will remember that information and flinch when heard in future.

The following eight aids to successful telephone selling and/or advertising give a good general idea of how to conduct such calls - and will be of assistance when selling and advertising generally.

A. DEVISE AN OPENING WITH INSTANT INTEREST WITH NO HIGH POWER PLOYS

"Good morning, I`m Henry from Grange Car Emporium and I`m delighted to tell you that our new premises open next Friday. We would be delighted if you would join us for a wine and cheese opening and, also, I`d like you to inspect our wide range of cars for sale..." The listener starts to demur. "That`s no problem, sir, no obligation to buy. We just hope that you will remember us the next time you change your car. So, think of the future and do come along..."

Henry telephoned because the listener had purchased his last car from the firm a year or so ago. Henry could have mentioned that useful fact in his introduction but decided to keep it up his sleeve and mention it later in the conversation. It might be a way of getting a fading discussion going again. Was he correct to do this? You consider the alternatives.

Henry made a good introduction. It`s friendly, informative and low key with no high powered sales talk to annoy the listener. It says, "OK, there`s always tomorrow and a drink and a nibble in the meantime". Such an approach should not upset the touchiest listener.

A way to lose immediate interest is to be far too friendly or matey. So often I have been completely put off a caller by hearing "How are you today?", "How are you doing?" or a similar inane question. It tells me that I am about to be subjected to some boring high-powered sales spiel. That puts me on my guard - the caller is losing fast.

A last thought on opening remarks. Consider this remark, "Do you want to be really rich?" Is that a good or poor opening? Think about it.

B. RING AT A CONVENIENT AND SENSIBLE TIME. YOU CAN`T COMPETE WITH A THRILLING WIMBLEDON FINAL

Graham Bell made it possible for us to be telephoned at inconvenient times.

It is essential to always telephone at a convenient time - that is, convenient to the listener not to you. Avoid the times when the listener may have a mouthful of steak and kidney pie. A call at lunch time will nearly always be met with, "...Sorry, I haven`t the time right now...I`m busy..." You apologise and immediately get off the line. There is no point in pushing your luck. Try later at a more convenient time.

If it is sensed that the listener is trying to put you off by saying that he is busy you have to accept that situation. You apologise and say, "Will you have a few minutes to talk if I call you tomorrow...say, at four o`clock?" That is polite and should ensure a positive answer, even if it just to get you off the line. That will be excellent for, when calling tomorrow, it will not be a cold call and you could say, "I`m phoning as arranged..." That will remind the listener that he agreed to your call. You are nearly a friend and have a foot in the door.

C. RELAX – BE YOURSELF; BE EVERYDAY.

No gimmicks. No business jargon. No annoying sales spiel. Just talk as you do everyday and you will sound both natural and genuine. That is the right approach with any hope of success. That will encourage the receiver to make observations. The caller (you) will be easily understood and have created a rapport. Remember you can so easily pass on your feelings to a listener - be half-hearted and he will reflect that mood; so, be enthusiastic about your business and carry the competitor with you.

D. BE PROFESSIONAL NOT AMATEURISH

Do not give the listener the chance of thinking, "What a load of old rubbish. He doesn`t know what he is talking about. I`ve had enough". The telephone is slammed down. You really do deserve that fate if the impression is given that you are "out of your depth".

You must convince that you really know what you are talking about. Always thoroughly research and be capable of discussing in an interesting manner every aspect of the business in hand. Never say, "I`m sorry I don`t know…" That is a deplorable admission of defeat. Of course, you will occasionally be confronted with a difficult question that you cannot answer. Then, you must aim to be helpful and offer a solution. "That is a most interesting and unusual question. I`ve never thought of it that way. I will ascertain the answer and call you back". Who could be offended at that approach? You must only use that technique when confronted with an unusual question; never to hide your lack of being able to answer a question that someone in your position should be able to deal with. In those other circumstances you will have to talk intelligently - not waffle! - around the question making sure that you do not sink deeper into the mire. Be brief and do not bring into your answer any matter which is controversial. Put the question to sleep as soon as possible.

E. NO "ER`S OR AH`S" – SUCH HESITATIONS SOUND AWFUL OVER THE TELEPHONE

Do not get lost in the middle of a call. It is useful to jot down a list of the points that you intend to make. Just a few words or phrases as reminders will be sufficient. Obviously the conversation will not follow the list. You will be side-tracked. Nevertheless, the note will serve its purpose; it will help to keep your thoughts together. You will find it useful to briefly list answers to awkward questions that may be put to you. Copy the TV newsreaders who look and act as if their fluency is natural and unprompted. TV viewers do not notice the prompter. A listener cannot see you but he can hear and will detect whether you are confident and truthful.

To have some notes before creates confidence and will stop you straying from the main purpose of the call.

F. ALWAYS GET A FORWARD COMMITMENT

With all calls - especially a cold call - it is desirable to get a commitment from the potential customer. Do not inconclusively and weakly end on, "That's OK., I'll 'phone you tomorrow". Be constructive. "Thanks, for listening to me. Let us arrange a date for a future talk. I'll 'phone you at two o'clock next Tuesday. Is that convenient to you? In the meantime do consider (name the goods or services you are endeavouring to sell); you will realise that they are exceptional value".

Without a commitment you are likely to start the next call in an uncertain manner, "Hello, Mr Williams...I called you last week...you were busy...well, I thought I would 'phone again..." You get the point; there is no common ground to commence a conversation. It is virtually another cold call.

G. ONE FACE-TO-FACE MEETING IS SO MUCH BETTER THAN MANY MOUTH-TO-EAR DISCUSSIONS

If appropriate - and in nearly all negotiations it will be - get a face-to-face meeting. It should not be too difficult to arrange, say, "Don't you agree, Mr Williams, that it would help us both if I called on you? I would like to meet you and have a few minutes together. How about ten minutes together on Friday? Let's allow fifteen minutes for our chat". That is a positive approach and you commit the competitor to only fifteen minutes of his valuable time. That period can be stretched out if needs be. If that time is not convenient to Mr Williams let him suggest an alternative. You will quickly perceive if you are talking to a genuine potential customer or whether it is time to move onto greener pastures.

Always remember - endeavour to get a face-to-face meeting to do business. That is the best way of getting a true understanding with customers-to-be.

H. ALWAYS BE POLITE – EVEN IF MET WITH ABUSE

When cold calling it is vital to remember you are making a call and imposing on another person without his permission or any advance word of warning. You will be met with all sorts of comments, some pleasant, some unpleasant and some really abusive. You must not compete in any way with rudeness or sly remarks. Let them wash over you like water off a duck's back. To get into a slanging match will get you nowhere - it certainly won't get you sales! However, if you are getting nowhere and you sense that the competitor just hates being approached by sales people it is sensible to call it a day, politely take leave and put the 'phone down. I consider that being rude or swearing at a person puts **YOUR** blood pressure up and that is not a wise action in any circumstances.

SELLING AND ADVERTISING ON THE TELEPHONE is tough work but properly used it can be very successful. It takes you direct to a potential or existing customer at very little cost. You will have many setbacks and many telephones will be slammed down as you talk. Then, give yourself a pep talk. Act confidently and you will soon have turned many potential customers into real money spending ones. But it will always be hard work...

11
ARE YOU BEING SUCCESSFUL?

That is a fundamental question and the "bottom line" is the acid test. Nevertheless, it is advantageous to undertake a detailed analysis to show which media produces the best results and, at the same time, it will become apparent what percentage of callers are turned into valuable customers spending hard cash - and that is, of course, the absolute test and the only reason why advertising takes place.

From their own commercial experience advertisers and business persons will know the best way to reach their potential customers but demand is an ever changing fashion. The average person gains experience from both natural instinct and by intelligent observation. I am leaving aside the qualitative market research methods as used by large firms as those are outside the scope of this book. Knowledge acquired by intelligent observation of both every day and commercial life is of great value to the advertiser. If gathered and correctly used it is his life blood.

A tip-top composer of displays only gains that status by analysing and learning from **ALL** past experience. Never forget that you probably learn more from your own mistakes than from your greatest hits. So, to obtain continuous success the demand produced by past advertising campaigns must be fastidiously scrutinised. You must be continuously thinking, "Did that last display really reach sufficient potential customers and how many were converted into actual buyers?" How do you answer that question? To have the answer is to have at your fingertips the most accurate guide to profitably to help your present and future programmes. There is nothing as valuable as having reliable figures that show the money produce by past displays. You will then know whether or not your advertising is successful. Therefore, it is essential that considerable thought is given as to how those figures can be obtained. It is useful to know how the more recent displays have fared in the marketplace for the supply and demand for goods and services can so quickly change and the sooner you are aware of any change the better.

In certain types of business it is relatively easy to ascertain the source of potential customers. In an estate agent's office or car showrooms many callers enquire direct as a result of an advertisement cut from a newspaper. The sales person or assistant should be asked to note such information so that the sales manager can have prepared a weekly or monthly summary. Also, any interesting comments made by potent customer should be relayed to the sales manager as those comments may help the drafter when preparing future displays and the management when reviewing general policy.

A weekly or monthly summary - whichever time span suits the business - is a useful tool and is an important guide. It takes little time to compose and yet is a helpful basic planning tool. This following suggested layout is a basic summary sheet and many items may be added to suit individual businesses.

SUMMARY SHEET for week x

No of callers to showrooms - 93 (Note: This number only contains one person when he is accompanied by others)

No of 'phone calls from displays - 74 (Note: It may not be possible to arrive at a meaningful figure and whether or not this item will be of benefit will be decided by the management)

CASUAL CALLERS - 48

Cars sold **NEW** 2xMegane Coupe 1xFord KA
          NOT NEW 2xFord KA

BY RECOMMENDATIONS - CALLERS 9

Cars sold   **NEW** 1xBMW 520 Sports

PAST CUSTOMERS - CALLERS 4

Cars sold **NEW** 1xBMW Mini
          NOT NEW 1xFord Fiesta

FROM EVENING POST - CALLERS 14

Cars sold **NEW** 4xFord KA   2xFord Fiesta 1xBMW Mini

FROM COUNTY GAZETTE - CALLERS 7
Cars sold   **NEW** 2xBMW 520 Sports

Customer's comments: 14 callers were only interested in BMW cars. 20 callers interested in only low priced not new cars.

Over a period of time good or bad results/ publicity will show up. Response and demand from the public is never static so these summary sheets can help to recognise and interpret shifts. If similar trends shown in this summary sheet were repeated over, say, eight weeks of trading the sales manager would make these observations:

1 Most callers are from The Evening Post. Cheaper range of cars sold through it. Would it increase business to advertise two days each week instead of one? Now display every Thursday when the Motor Section of the paper appears. Would additional expenditure on the Thursday be more beneficial that advertising on a second day in the week? Note: All other motor traders display on the Thursday only.

2 Limited number of callers from The County Gazette, although it consistently produces two or three sales of higher value cars each month. Coverage includes more affluent areas of the town. Keep weekly display based on BMW cars.

3 Excellent number of sales to casual callers. This indicates that the showrooms are in a splendid prominent position which invites passers-by to pop in when passing. Although eight weeks figures should not lead to far-reaching decisions, a much longer record of callers and sales could lead to these considerations - would renovating the front of the premises make them even more eye-catching and increase callers? Next door premises are coming up for sale next month; would make an excellent and very visible extension to existing premise. Speak to the boss about these two matters; he will know whether it would be economic to expand.

General comment: you will realise how trends detected through advertisements and the analysis of results can assist when considering the future of a business and, perhaps more to the point, your own future career.

Clearly, the close examination of how and why advertisements are either effective or ineffective will produce a wide variety of interesting and potentially profitable ideas. That is why time is not wasted undertaking this exercise. Ignore this aspect of research and you career or business may well drift like a rudderless ship. There will be little to guide it towards continuing profitability.

In a business with a quick turnover it will be somewhat more difficult to collect this vital information. This will include any comments from customers. The manager must rely on the observations of staff who should be asked to report daily with any useful tips received. If advised in advance of special displays, sales staff being in direct contact with customers will be able to help the manager to correctly ascertain results. Displays producing outstanding business speak for themselves and no inquest is necessary; but a sales manager must still be inquisitive and look for ways to improve. There is nearly always a way to better even the most brilliant success.

The man-in-the-street with an item to sell and the greatest businesses in the UK rely on advertisements in one way or another. It is only possible to be and remain successful if the drafter knows and acts on both the good and bad results of the past. Nothing, it is said, succeeds like success. Let us alter that adage so it becomes one of the guiding principles of advertising –

ADVERTISING SUCCEEDS WHEN IT IS BUILT ON PAST SUCCESSES

12
A BRIEF RESUME – WHY ADVERTISE?

Before considering that vital job of drafting advertisements it will be useful to have a brief look at why it is necessary to advertise. You have seen all the hard work necessary to achieve really skilled profitable drafts. You may well ask is it imperative to go to all that bother? Why advertise? Week-by-week or month-by-month you have agonised as you draft all those - what seem to you - gems. Yet, you have come to consider it a chore, a complete bore and a waste of both valuable time and money. You have plodded on thinking that someone has to do it. Therefore, with all those wild thoughts running through your mind it is crucial to illustrate why that weekly/monthly task is an indispensable part of your job or of your business and of your ultimate success. Thereafter, you may not regret the constant task of drafting those world beating displays!

There are so many reasons why it is necessary to advertise and the most interesting ones are grouped under the following five headings:

1 WHY ADVERTISE? - BECAUSE IT IS AN ESSENTIAL ELEMENT OF THE WIDE BUSINESS WORLD.

That is fair enough. It means that buyers and sellers must advertise to comply with the "rules of the game". If they did not do so they would be the odd persons out and lose both prestige and business. To play on a level playing field they must do as their competitors do - but, even better! A trader may not want to spend money on advertising but he must make a virtue of necessity and comply with convention. However, alongside the reason under this heading is the most practical inducement which is given under the next heading.

2 WHY ADVERTISE? - BECAUSE IT IS USED BY ALL COMPETITORS.

The following example will illustrate why you must toe the line and advertise.

Mr Gatelio has an Italian restaurant on the edge of the heart of the main leisure area in a south coast seaside resort. He is a little on the mean side and decides to save money by not advertising. It seemed so easy to make that extra profit and he rubs his hands in anticipation of a healthier bottom line to the accounts.

Mr Gatelio`s restaurant is in direct competition with many other eating places in and around that leisure centre and there are four well-established ones actually in the leisure centre. He knows that all the other owners advertise in many different ways - for example, in the local newspapers, in the tourist guide, on the local authority`s map displayed in the leisure centre and when a hungry tourist pushes the name button of a competitor a light pinpoints that restaurant...and so on. By advertising his competitors cream off a large percentage of the available business particularly parties which are booked in advance from displays in the local press. After the first six weeks of the summer season Mr Gatelio is worried for looking back on the same period last year his takings are twenty-seven per cent down. Mrs G - who is the real brains of the partnership - pleads with him to "do just a little advertising".

Mr Gatelio must be more realistic and accept that advertising is part and parcel of everyday business - it is being successfully used by all his competitors and won`t go away. He must realise that his restaurant is on the edge of the main leisure area and needs boosting more than the busier ones actually in the leisure area. He must accept the inevitable or his restaurant will fail. Readers will be relieved to know that Mrs G won and her husband reluctantly organised some advertising; more customers appeared and the year turned out to be fairly successful - although the loss over the non-advertising period was not fully made up.

Leaving Mr Gatelio to his obviously new urge to advertise here is a real life reason why traders must advertise. The public (potential customers) expect firms to advertise. Many years ago I worked for a firm of estate agents who, for some reason or another, decided to cease advertising. That is bizarre behaviour for any estate agent. The public immediately picked-up that the firm did not have their usual displays in the local newspapers. They expected it and instructions from owners who wanted to sell their homes dramatically fell away. Few owners wanted to put their business in the hands of the firm.

The non-advertising policy was definitely the reason for the fall in instructions to sell properties. The public told us that in no uncertain terms. Advertising was recommenced and instructions to sell properties regained their lost momentum. That was sure proof that advertising really paid. That may well be an extreme example as estate agents` displays are a commonplace sight in the local press. However, it does illustrate how observant the general public can be. The lesson is this - never underestimate the shrewdness of the public. Do so and you are will be the loser.

3   WHY ADVERTISE? - TO REMAIN IN BUSINESS

The lesson of this heading ties in with (1) and (2) above. Namely, if your displays do not appear alongside competitor`s displays you will be forced into advertising to attract business and in the final analysis to remain in business.  To stop advertising to save money - or, for any other reason - is like locking the shop`s door. The message is this - whether times are easy or hard your name and business **MUST** be kept before the public. Let potential customers see that you are open for business.

4   WHY ADVERTISE? - IT IS ESSENTIAL TO INCREASE BUSINESS

Each and every one of your competitors who are trying to increase business will find it very hard work, it is a constant grind to expand...and that, of course, includes you and your firm or your employers. Are you able to think of a new way of coming to the notice of a wider audience? First-rate goods and services with realistic pricing is one of the best ways to increase turnover and profitability. That is fine but you must go out into the wider world and seek **NEW** customers. They are not likely to be sitting on your doorstep waiting for you. The only way to be seen and/or heard in that wider world is to make the public aware of you and your business. You must go to them and the only realistic way of doing that is to advertise in all its forms. Successful traders will be constantly revising their advertising policy in scope, design and wording. That is the way - the only way - to increase business. Conversely, do not forget that whether you produce goods or supply services your actual business must keep up with your advertising. It is pointless spending money and time on more advertising if you are unable to supply the extra goods or services. There must be a balance between what the business is capable of producing for sale and the scope of the advertising campaign. If, for example, the displays are producing more customers than can be supplied, then increase production. It is essential to get that balance about right.

5 WHY ADVERTISE? – BECAUSE IT PRODUCES BUSINESS

Advertisers have been displaying their products and services for many, many years. If advertising did not work it would have died out long ago - like the Dodo. Shrewd persons never waste time and money on a futile activity. Furthermore, it can be seen that it truly works if the figures on the "bottom line" are healthy. Those figures never lie. Of course, you must be careful when analysing those bottom line figures for there may be other unconnected factors that have an impact on them. However, those figures and the Summary Sheets will help to ascertain the result of advertising that has been undertaken.

Suppose, just for a moment or two that your advertising did not work. All your displays failed to bring in money-spending customers, you would ask yourself - why? It could be one of three reasons. Firstly, your displays are of poor quality and have virtually no pulling power. They are completely lost amongst a multitude of far better ones. Secondly, your goods or services are inferior to those of competitors and/or are overpriced. Thirdly, potential customers are receiving inferior service from the telephonists and/or the sales staff.

You see, the problem is not advertising, per se. It is your hands to ascertain the reason for poor sales and to make sure that it is dealt with pdq. Do not rush in and blame advertising for it is well-known from the experience of millions of businesses that advertising does work. Remember that old adage - bad workmen always blame their tools. If it is correctly ascertained that the first reason (poor advertising) is why business is falling away then face up to it; you drafted the displays so you are to blame. Then, no adage or excuse will help you. After due consideration alter your advertising style and wording and move on.

From the above five answers it will be realised that advertising is a necessity. Make a virtue of that necessity and get down to it in a proper professional manner. You will never regret it.

13
ON DRAFTING ADVERTISEMENTS

You`ve got to accentuate the positive,
Eliminate the negative...
> (From a popular 1940`s song)

It will be beneficial to recall that advertisements have only one real purpose - to motivate the reader and/or the listener and to put some money into the pocket of the advertiser. It is useful to know a little about motivation. It can be defined in a single sentence - motivation is that force which impels a person to action. That is a straightforward definition and it means so much to all advertisers. It is just what you desire of all readers or listeners from all your displays - **ACTION.** It follows that in order to achieve that desired state you must ascertain why your readers unknowingly want to do what you are trying to make them do.

Consider - your advertisement is to sell bicycles. It must be put into a reader`s mind that he **MUST** buy a bike. However, that is not quite enough. The question that you must endeavour to ask is this - **WHY** does he want a bike? Again, that is not quite enough. To the advertiser the elusive question is - how can I persuade (motivate) the reader that life is impossible unless he owns a bike? An example, the advertisement is a giant poster at the junction of two very busy main roads. There is always a traffic jam at that junction at peak times. The poster must tell the reader why a bike must be purchased. It states boldly that riding a bike saves all the hassle of traffic jams. This particular reader is a young person who is perfectly able to cycle to and from work, yet he sits in that same traffic jam nearly every morning and early evening. With little else to do he glances at the poster and suddenly thinks, "Hi...a great idea...I`m so tired of all these wretched traffic jams. I`ll buy a bike...I`ll cycle to work. That poster did the trick. It persuaded - motivated - that young person and he did just what the poster demanded.

Of course, it is not always easy to ascertain that vital yet elusive "why"? It is often obtained by detailed market research. But do not despair you can do much to ascertain some of the motives of your potential customers. The person running a small/medium firm is much nearer his customers than the advertising department of a large firm. That person will be able to talk directly to customers and to have face-to-face discussions giving direct views of customer's thoughts and desires. Those views are of the utmost importance and must be considered when drafting displays. It is reasonable to assume that what attracted existing customers is likely to motivate potential customers. A discussion with existing customers is never a waste of time and can often help as new products and ideas can be put before them.

WHAT MAKES A REALLY GOOD ADVERTISER?

The first lesson under this heading is that you must be an **OPPORTUNIST PAR EXCELLENCE.** As such you will always strike whilst the iron is hot and will not be a slave to rules or everyday regulations. If you always advertise on a Friday and on the Saturday you have numerous unsold goods get onto the local press and persuade the powers that be to put a display in Monday's paper and endeavour to get your money in some days earlier...do not wait for the following Friday as you will have other goods to advertise on that day. An opportunist grabs business today; he makes a decision today and acts pdq. That type of action makes a first-class advertiser.

A tip - learn from both the finest and the inferior. It must be repeated that anyone aspiring to draft top-flight displays must spend time reading and listening to other advertisers' ventures. You will very soon pick out those that attract you. The well-thought out and the well-presented ones that you feel would motivate you to action.

It will be of greater benefit to be able to identify what you consider to be poor displays; those that you feel have no motivating force. Watch out for those that are repeats of last week's failed displays and the drafter has not made the time or doesn't have the energy to compose worthwhile displays that sell. That person is either incompetent or lazy, probably both. You will learn from those displays and will avoid making the same errors. It is interesting to note that other person's mistakes have a habit of remaining in your mind and the lessons that you learn will not easily go away. Other person's mistakes are good for you!

Gather together ideas for your Ideas Book and do not be shy of collecting together a list of all those bad examples. To have a personal record in the Ideas Book will help you to recall pitfalls/traps. To be forewarned is to be forearmed.

LOOK FOR A PERSON'S BASIC NEED

What are the basic needs and desires of the man-in-the-street; that elusive man who travels on the Clapham omnibus. In fact, those yearnings are possessed by all persons from the poorest in the land to the most wealthy. A sense of belonging to a family must be top of the list. Have you noticed how ecstatic a daughter is when a TV presenter brings on the mother not seen for some twenty-five years? High on the list of desires is belonging to the local community in which one lives. Isn't it pleasant to be greeted in the street or in the local supermarket by a friend? Very high in the list is economic well-being and security. Being secure in a job is nearly everyone's wish. People do like to be recognised for what they are and do. A plumber loves to hear that he is an excellent plumber. Likewise, in all businesses and trades we like to be seen as competent in our work. There are many aspirations and those mentioned above are probably the most popular ones. All of those needs and desires can be reflected in your displays. In fact, they are the grist to the advertiser's mill. That is, to alter a hackneyed phrase, food for both considerable thought and use.

These four basic principles are inherent in competent advertising:

ORIGINAL*BRIEF* DESCRIPTIVE*HONEST

As a test of this statement open a newspaper or magazine. Take the first display that catches your eye and you will immediately detect its compliance with those fundamental components - and that was why that display caught your eye. That is a lesson to learn.

BE ORIGINAL

This is the pre-requisite to high-class advertising of magnetic quality; it produces that first and lasting impression which both attracts and pulls in the maximum number of potential customers. Lord Byron said, "Maidens like moths, are ever caught by glare" to which advertisers might add"...and so are customers". Did not the great Picasso achieve fame by being both a fine artist and for being original? Probably his originality was the attribute that caused his worldwide fame. There is a lesson in that last sentence.

So, be bold, be uninhibited and do not be frightened of pioneering. Originality is being new and fresh. Keep well away from the certain trap of being a mere copyist of stereotype advertisements. That trap is already brimful of average and (well) below average exponents of tedium.

As an extreme illustration of how originality helped to create fame consider the work of another outstanding painter. Think of the posters designed and painted by Toulouse Lautrec. In the late 1890`s when he haunted all the night spots of the Montmartre his paintings of the gay dancing girls at the Moulin Rouge aroused immense interest. The originality of his bright and colourful, flat and angular figures startled and greatly impressed his audiences. Even to this day his name is linked to the Moulin Rouge and both individually and collectively are worldwide famous. That illustrates how originality created a first and lasting impression of both the originator (the artist) and his work.

Being original does not mean being outlandish. If your displays stray too far from the conventional many readers will be completely lost; the average reader is reasonably bright but few geniuses read the classified advertisements or more than just glance at posters. It is a sound rule that if you are personally excited about a draft it is likely to excite others. However, that is not enough evidence to prove that you have produced a winner. Test the idea on your wife, other relations, friends, business colleagues and so on. Then, with their comments in mind have another close look at the idea. In view of the comments received - can it be approved? If you receive a blast of negative comments do beware as a group of ordinary people in the street are not with you. Those are the people that you must attract. Never be obstinate and refuse to act on reliable advice even when it contradicts your own views. Do not forget that on occasions you could be wrong - now, that is a sobering thought.

Being original is telling it straight. How many advertisers do that? I must admit that I cannot see the point of some displays on the TV, particularly when the subject matter relates to cars. I wonder what the pictures and actions on screen have to do with the car being advertised. To me, those obscure displays are not playing it straight. You must get the message over to the potential customer in an original and uncluttered way, in a way that will be clearly understood. Cut out all the clever clutter. You must attract (motivate) potential customers, not convince yourself of your own cleverness. Look at it this way - call a spade a spade, do not advertise a spade as a spatha which suddenly, just before the close of the display, becomes a spade. Look at many of the displays on the TV screen - especially advertising cars - and you will soon realise the lesson being conveyed in this paragraph.

BE BRIEF

The slow and unhurried tempo of the past has gone and with it all those wordy advertisements. The viewer of a newspaper display or of a poster only has time to glance at it as he rushes headlong into the future. It is the draftsman's job to arrest, just for a flash, that rush and to register a more lasting impression in the observer's mind. Then or later the observer will return to the advertiser's message and may well become a potential customer. It is pointless to try to reason why the brain suddenly flashes back and remembers a past event. All that matters to an advertiser is that it does often happen particularly if the event was a little out of the ordinary. Somewhere in the brain it rested until some thought or happening caused the event to reappear as a brainwave that the observer considers must be investigated. The display is just beginning to work and the observer is coming under its influence. Be that as it may, it is now opportune to consider how an advertisement can have that delayed effect on the reader or listener.

The allure of a few well selected words, pictures or simple symbols is all that is needed to arrest that rush. Paul Valery said, "Advertising has annihilated the power of most adjectives". That is true, so why use what is unnecessary? Let the reader or listener see the wood for the trees, so away with all that useless verbiage. Estate agents are the worst offenders as it seems that all properties are attractive, magnificent or exceptional except, of course, the charming, unique or impressive ones. Recently in a glossy magazine I counted twelve "attractive" and "very attractive" properties in only five pages of displays. I close my eyes and count to ten every time I read that a house is "well-situated". As it is said that familiarity breeds contempt, it is a waste of effort, time and money.

So, brevity attracts attention. To acquire it ruthlessly cut out all the prattle. Use short staccato sentences to convey the message. Say it, keep to it and move on. You will soon realise that in advertising suggestion is more tantalising to readers and listeners than a rigid obvious statement.

A lesson to learn - keep it short and simple. Prove that you are a good writer of copy and do not attempt to show with words or pictures that you are a genius. Carefully read your drafts and unclutter the clutter.

An example of bad advertising is provided by estate agents who try to attract attention by introducing a local scene onto their for sale boards. It does not work and goes against the basic rule of sensible advertising - keep displays uncluttered. A background creates a visual muddle. A simple for sale board with the agent`s name, telephone number and e-mail address is all that the reader wants to see. That is a splendid example of an uncluttered and brief display. It is easy to read as the potential buyer rushes by.

Lastly, some words which make an apt summary to this subject of being brief. They were spoken by that very wise man Sir Winston Churchill, "The Treasury paper by its very length, defends itself against the risk of being read". What a wonderful sentence.

BE DESCRIPTIVE

Advertisements must be descriptive in words as well as in pictures or symbols. They must have appeal, be alive and be interesting. A bald statement, "Buy Blogg's Coffee" will not arouse a second glance. But, the caption, "I've come 4, 043 miles just for you" will cause many a head to turn and see under that statement a coffee bean from Brazil jumping into your coffee pot - by courtesy of Bloggs. You see originality and being descriptive go hand-in-hand.

Some years ago there was a poster whose message was so accurately conveyed to the reader that there were objections to its use. It was temporarily banned but later became one of the true great posters of all time and its influence is still with us. Its dramatic descriptive message played a big part in the road safety campaign. It complied with all four basic advertisement principles - it was original, brief, descriptive and honest. Yet only five words were used - Keep Death off the Road. That slogan is put under this heading as no slogan is so descriptive.

When a display includes a photograph, illustration or a symbol it must be remembered that when reproduced in a newspaper, on a poster, in a mail shot and so on the image must be clear. Take a look at the property illustrations in the local press. Many are mediocre and so poor that it can be seen that the house is detached and that is about all. Wording alone could do better than those pitiful pictures. How many pictures will force the reader to take action and to telephone the estate agent for further details and an appointment to view? Maybe the wording under the picture will help to spark some interest. Furthermore, any poor picture, illustration or symbol is rotten publicity and it reflects badly on the advertiser's overall publicity. It is fair to state that the poor quality of the picture may not be the fault of the advertiser. With some newspapers the paper used does not seem to be suitable for photographic reproductions. This is noticed with small photograph. However, as already stated, a bad workman blames his tools. You should ascertain the likely result of using pictures before doing so. Call and discuss your proposal with the Advertising Manager of the newspaper you will be using. If in any doubt play it safe - keep too easy to read and understand words. Remember - one clear sentence beats many poor pictures.

Under this heading it is useful to consider whether address panels and pre-paid addresses are useful to attract potential customers. Both are used as inducements to persuade a reader that he can respond to the display with little effort and, in the latter case, at no expense.

Firstly, is it a plus point to have a coupon or label in an advertisement so that readers can easily complete it and return it to the trader? I consider that its use is debatable. At least the advertiser will know that the reader has been motivated to buy a stamp! The only way to ascertain whether or not this method of promotion will benefit you is to have a trial run. A question for you to consider - wouldn't you rather have a potential customer telephoning so that he can be spoken to on a personal basis? It does depend on the size of the business; the smaller the business the more beneficial it is to have personal customers who become well-known to the staff. A pre-paid telephone number on selected displays could become costly but consider this inducement - is it worth a trial run?

Secondly, is it beneficial to use a pre-paid address in a display? Will it help to compel a reader to take action? It will not cost him a penny. If a person has to pay to contact an advertiser doesn't it show that he is more interested in the goods than someone who hasn't paid a penny? Who knows? If you are tempted to use a pre-paid address have a trial run. Again it depends on the size of the business and the distance of operation from base. Potential customers living near an advertiser are more likely to make a personal call or telephone than those living further away from the advertiser's business. The larger the business the more convenient it could be to have a mass of pre-paid replies than many telephone calls that it may be hard to deal with in an efficient manner.

The two matters raised in the last two paragraphs do present many questions that still remain unanswered. They are included in this section as may, in the right circumstances, be of beneficial use. The remarks given are a general guide only and to question whether the methods are worth your use; however, do conduct a careful trial run before permanently use.

BE HONEST

There are legal and moral reasons why honesty is the best and only policy. An advertisement may be dishonest without being illegal and that is the type of display that comes under this heading. Such a display may be misleading or extravagant in its claims.

Those readers who have read Boswell`s Life of Johnson may call Mrs Thrale saying, "I do not know for certain what will please Dr Johnson, but I do know for certain that it will displease him to praise anything, even that which he like, extravagantly". That`s a splendid lesson to learn. Even what the doctor liked he did not want to praise extravagantly. Therein lies a lesson for all those who draft advertisements.

The man-in-the-street is bound to be suspicious of the ecstatic over-praise often associated with selling. He will turn away from a string of euphoric adjectives. His reaction is likely to be - no goods or services are that super...just another catch penny. So, another potential customer is lost. The words and pictures in all displays must ring true when the wares are inspected. If a car is said to be "in immaculate condition", when in reality it is barely in fair shape, viewers will be put off and angry on wasting time and money. That trader will not be visited again. That is bad enough but damage to the trader`s reputation can be further damaged when the infuriated viewer tells relations, friends, et al. of his horrible experience. Of course, the tale worsens as it is passed on. Dishonesty does lose today`s trade and much future business.

To quote Shakespeare, who appears to have the advertiser in mind when writing his plays, "An honest tale speeds best, being plainly told". Isn`t that true of first-class advertising? In fact, it is often policy to undersell so that the viewer is thrilled to find the goods in superior condition and/or of better value than suggested in the blurb. That will create a tremendous amount of goodwill and the buyer may well become a regular customer and a true ambassador for the business. That is the ultimate aim of advertising. All in all, being honest makes good business sense and creates both customers and goodwill.

TO DRAFT TOP QUALITY DISPLAYS THAT RAISES THEM ABOVE THE LEVEL OF THE AVERAGE MARKETPLACE BE-

ORIGINAL * BRIEF * DESCRIPTIVE * HONEST

A word of warning - one of the worst mistakes that an advertiser can make is to invite readers to make an offer when a price is being quoted. Why tempt providence? Be bold and quote a firm price for you may obtain it.

"Car for sale - £10,000 or near offer" What does that mean? Only the draftsman knows. But, more to the point, its message to readers is clear - the seller does not have faith in his asking price and does not expect to receive the full price of £10,000. Even before anyone has inspected he has weakened his own position and shot himself in the foot. An interested party will invariably make an offer whether invited to do so or not. If offers are not invited any offers received can be refused by saying, "My price is £10,000, sorry I`m not open to offer". At the appropriate time, if needs be, after haggling and to clinch a deal the gesture can be made, "I didn`t intend to reduce my price but to close a deal **IMMEDIATELY** I will accept as the lowest price £9,500". Therefore, when composing an advertisement it is sound advice to quote a definite price and let any haggling take place from that strong position. Consider that position to one that would apply if the display invited an offer.

A seller requiring an urgent sale and willing to consider an offer less than the advertised price should quote that lower figure and widen the demand for his goods. I have a maxim that I keep constantly before me - the lower the quoting price the greater the chance of a sale. That is, of course, common sense but how often do we forget that and try complicated methods that do not work.

I consider that it is detrimental to creating interest by putting "no offers" in displays. That is likely to put off some readers who will not answer the display. That reader may reason, "There`s a person who won`t bargain. He wants £10,000 and my very top is £9,500.

That really is my maximum. I won`t waste any of my time". Another potential customer lost. "No offers" is put beside a price to show that the full price is required - no less. That is fine but who knows, that after some useless haggling the seller may get the customer to pay the full price. The objective must be to get the potential customer into conversation and then, if that is your desire, state that the asking price is not negotiable. So, do not let those two words "no offers" stop a reader answering the display.

Your car is advertised at £11,000 – no offers" and after seeing at least a dozen viewers it is still unsold. You realise that the price is too high and that you have a tricky problem. You either go back to some of those viewers and invite offers or advertise again. In both cases you are, to quote Hamlet, hoist by your own petard. You will find that all callers know of the old unrealistic price and you are on the wrong foot. You will, of course, receive silly offers as everyone loves a bargain. The task of selling your car at a realistic price has been made much more difficult. So, you see, the lesson is not to commit yourself so firmly when there is no need to do so.

If, despite the advice given above you do advertise goods with the tag "no offers" do not even hint that you may accept an offer. Make it seem that you are really going to abide by the words in your display. Let a potential buyer make the first move.

14

THE MOTIVATING FORCES – THE THEMES

You will now realise that a potential customer has to be motivated, that is inspired by the advertiser using a theme - in short, a ground for action. In order to do its job successfully the theme must be cast around a basic force that motivates human beings. There is no other way to motivate people.

The advertiser is fortunate as there are many motivating themes and a wide choice to suit differing circumstances. When considering these themes it is important to bear in mind that both the spending power and the age range of the targeted market must be taken into consideration. The drafter will know his customers and have a good idea of the theme that is likely to impel them to action. Here are the best known and most frequently used motivating forces:

SEX - I have often heard it stated that sex is the most motivating force for really magnetic advertising. That may be an exaggeration; nevertheless, it is without doubt a very strong basis desire and a constant and effective theme. A display that relies merely on the beauty queen image is now way out of date. Beauty - sex - getting what you want must nowadays all be linked. For example, the product being promoted will ensure that the man really gets the girl - or, vice versa. Many displays can be worked-up from that theme. As a general rule, this class of display has its greatest success through the mass media, particularly on the `web, on television, in Sunday newspapers, in weekly magazines and on posters. Most of those displays are put together by advertising agents.

ACQUIRING WEALTH - in Othello we read, "Poor and

content is rich and is rich enough". A fine sentiment but who today believes it? The urge to acquire money/wealth is second only to sex in motivation power. It is a common fallacy that wealth brings with it all the ingredients of happiness - yet, nearly everyone believes it to be so. In the displays the rich young man always gets the best looking girl although it may only be implied. So, screams the displays, if you do not have money buy our clothes, our cars, et al. and masquerade in the cloak of make-believe...by courtesy of our finance department. A wonderful second best! This theme may be used to show the reader or listener how to obtain wealth or, as an easier alternative, how to acquire that sham "moneyed look" without actually possessing the wherewithal to support it. To get rich is a common desire and any display that suggests to the reader that the advertised product might increase their wealth is a winner. Of course, it might win over the reader so that the desired action is taken but the crucial test is will it make him any wealthier? The first part of that last sentence is the only part that is of interest to the advertiser.

An advertisement that shows a celebrity wearing a certain brand of clothing will increase sales of that brand. The display motivates readers to believe that to look rich implies real wealth. So many people - especially the young - like to look like a celebrity and love to be seen as being "above their real station in life". These comments would equally be at home under the next heading - snobbery.

So, a very magnetic theme is wealth / money. It has wide appeal right across the community and used properly is a sure winner. Do not take my word for it; take a look at Country Life and all the County magazines.

SNOBBERY - So many people appear to be snobs or secret snobs and this theme has a wide appeal. It is used to persuade the reader that he really must possess a certain item so that friend, acquaintances, et al. are convinced that he belongs to a class higher than his true position in life. The real "he" or "she" is hiding behind a veneer of the imaginary class. He relishes the idea of being seen in that genteel false state. He and his type are splendid target for the advertiser.

Nowadays snobbery is a very powerful draw as celebrities rule the roost. It seems that everyone wants to be seen owning and wearing the up-to-the-minute fashions worn by those celebs. who haunt the TV screens, the newspapers and the glossy magazines. Look like a celeb. and you will be one - even if a large percentage of the population are wearing the same style of expensive sunglasses which, of course, the celeb. only wore once when filming for that TV display.

Let us now look at housing snobbery. People recklessly mortgage their future to live in a house that screams, "The owners have made it - just look at his house". Often the owner is struggling to keep up with the mortgage repayments and is dreading the next upward hike in interest rates. Never mind, the right image is being created and the advertiser is using him and his ilk to sell top-of-the-range cars, boats, furniture and other items that reinforce that upmarket image. Thank goodness, gloats the advertiser, that snobbery does exist.

You see that snobbery and snobs can help you to draft advertisements. There is a wealth of ideas under this heading. All the delusions of grandeur that you meet in life can be turned into ideas for the drafter's use. What a fantastic store of ideas for the Ideas Book. However, a caution, use this item surreptitiously as you must never even hint that a snob is a snob. Perish the thought!

A BARGAIN - Who doesn't gloat when a bargain is purchased? That is one of the most satisfying deals that a purchaser can make. An advertiser should rarely use the word "bargain" for the public do not believe the word when written by a trader. In any event, it cheapens the goods being sold. In many ways it implies that the advertiser is somewhat desperate and wants shot of the goods. Its over use and its dishonest use can turn a prospective purchaser away.

The way to tackle this problem is to concentrate on value. The words "below market value" or, better still, "below market value - compare our prices with our competitor's". The latter wording shows that the seller has real confidence and does not fear competition. The reader is actually being invited to look at competitor's goods and prices. The objective is to let the potential customer find out for himself that the advertiser is offering really good value - and that is real motivation.

It has been stated elsewhere that goods should always be advertised at the lowest possible price acceptable to the owner. The reason being that the lower the price the wider is the "really active" market. If, therefore, the advertised price is below true market value the opportunity is to tell the readers of the advertisements that that is so. Never knowingly say "...below market value..." when that is clearly not the case. That will get you nowhere and you will face a disappointed and angry potential customer when he inspects the goods. Another lost present and future customer.

GUILT - Announcements blare out, "Every wife desires...", "children just love...", "A house is not a home without" and many similar statements are made to make sure that the reader or listener feels guilty...until he remedies the guilt by doing what the advertisers want him to do. The message is ignored at his peril. The display is targeted at the wife, the children, the entire family... and the advertiser will leave them to complete the job. Of course, by persuasion and a little badgering the head of the household - the person in control of family finances - is likely to do as the display demands. The person who cannot comply with the message feels guilty, he has done his best for the family but...yes...of course... eventually he gives in.

LAZINESS - This theme does not only play on bone idleness but, also, on the exertion of less energy and/or the saving of time. To link both together is an admirable theme. It must be admitted that in this context most of us are, to a certain extent, lazy. Human energy and time are two most precious and irreplaceable commodities. Draftsmen using laziness as a theme will aim at a specific audience who spent much time and/or energy on certain activities. As examples, housewives in their kitchens, gardeners, men shaving, do-it-yourself enthusiasts decorating their own homes, et al...is just a few of the people who may be susceptible to displays playing on this theme. The message is simple - the jobs can be carried out "much quicker and with less effort so buy...(product name)...and save energy and time"...and other inducements to persuade the jaded housewife and the tired worker to become less jaded and tired. This is a very effective theme.

FAMILY LIFE - This very popular theme is probably used more than any other theme and in many different ways. The picture of a happy couple and two smiling kids comes quickly and easily to mind. Family life and the theme of guilt can together form a most powerful inducement - see Guilt theme above. It is an indisputable fact that the family (friendly) war creates far more consumer demand than the battle of the sexes. Family life embraces the property lived in, the furniture and effects used therein, the gardens, the cars, the jobs that the family do to earn their daily bread, the kid's schooling, the leisure time in the evenings and at weekends, the annual holidays, the home at Christmas...and very many more activities and functions. What an enormous pool in which to fish for ideas. As an exercise, you are a trader in fabrics dealing mainly in ready-made and made-to-order curtains. Draft two displays featuring family life and put those ideas in the Ideas Book for future use.

AN INVITATION - We are all inquisitive either through a general desire for knowledge or through plain nosiness. Both can usefully be used in the form of an invitation. Think about, "Come to the great sale at...", "Brighton invites you...", "You are welcome to our sale of...", "Visit the largest antique showrooms in..." and you can think of many more. These and similar statements rouse curiosity. Who can resist the invitation to see "the greatest...", "the largest..." or, indeed, anything that is a little out of the ordinary? But draftsmen beware there must be an element of truth in your invitations.

The more personal the draftsman makes the invitation the more likely it is to be accepted. Who can resist an invitation that includes a freebie? - a drink and a piece of cheese always helps to pull people in. I know from personal experience that when opening a show house on a new estate more people come for the freebies than to seriously consider buying one of the new houses.

A LINK WITH WELL-KNOWN PLACES

Familiar places and faces create a feeling of both permanency and well-being, an illusion that all is well. Consider these - Big Ben, Buckingham Palace, The Eiffel Tower, The White House, The Empire

State Buildings, The Kremlin, the Royal Pavilion at Brighton and so on. These well-known and loved landmarks are likely to be there for many thousands of tomorrows. As picture backgrounds for the appropriate advertisements there is added that little extra assurance that finally convince the reader that, as an example, shoes by Footerbetter rarely wear out. The reader will not realise that the background picture has set the scene and all is well and will be for aeons to come. The Footerbetter shoes are purchased in a glow of expectancy.

The theory is the same with faces. Subconsciously the reader muses that if the famous crooner recommends Wellwear sports jackets those items must be first-class; he won't let his name be used unless the jackets were really superb - would he? The reader is more convinced by the advertiser's ploy than the jackets being advertised.

This theme is very successfully used in a local context. Consider - the domes of the Royal Pavilion at Brighton; the White Cliffs of Dover; Robin Hood and Nottingham; the pier at Wigan - or lack of it made famous by George Orwell...these and hundreds like them can be exploited in local publicity. A good display to cover a local town is one featuring a local attraction or a well-known and loved local building. Local people have a great love for their local amenities and particularly for a feature that is well-known and loved across the nation. There is much scope for interesting and profitable displays within this theme.

Local newspapers are a useful media for displays that feature a local attraction. In the main these are read by local people who will appreciate and warm to displays showing a well-known local building, park, river, lake and so on. A local feature that is locally loved is grist to the mill of local advertising.

Many local persons prefer to do business in their local town. It helps local employment and keeps money within the community. That is another angle to exploit under this theme.

LUXURY - This theme gives so much scope to the draftsman and can be exploited in many ways. However, **REAL LUXURY** is generally exploited on the TV, on the internet, in glossy magazines, in County magazines and in some Sunday newspapers. The ordinary everyday so-called luxuries are advertised in virtually all media but avoid the really expensive ones.

REAL luxuries are those that only the wealthy can afford; **EVERYDAY** luxuries are treats that the rest of the community enjoy on occasions when there is a little cash to spare. The difference is fundamental as the advertising of real luxuries is a specialist subject and generally the province of the advertising agency. Furthermore, as real luxuries are expensive there is more capital available to use on publicity and advertising.

We would all just love a life of real luxury but very few succeed in that desire. Nevertheless, most of us have at least a little luxury in our lives. It is the draftsman's job to hold out the hope of a little more. There are varying degrees of luxury. To some it is sitting watching the sport on TV on a Saturday afternoon and being free of the stresses and worries of the working week; at the other extreme it is dining at the Ritz wearing a model dress by Dolce & Gabbana with expensive jewellery from Boodle & Dunthorne. Between these two extremes is an abundance of situations for the keen and perceptive draftsman to exploit. Luxury is like beauty it is the eye of the beholder and covers a wide spectrum of "must haves". As always, the draftsman's job is to is to use that "must have" to attract potential customers to his wares.

Many varieties of luxury can be used to attract the attention of the readers of advertisements. On the appeal to the great majority a comparatively pleasure is displayed as a luxury. There is the cigar after a hard day's work, the beauty relaxing in the bubble bath, the warmth of a real coal fire and so on. When the cigar and the bath are finished and the fire dies away the illusion of luxury quickly disappears. Nevertheless, it is an honest display and served its purpose. The reader buys the goods and enjoys a glimpse of the good life - should he expect more?

Real luxury can be used to appeal to the select few who can really afford to pay its price. A fine piece of Faberge jewellery is sold by displaying a fabulous Rolls Royce; the Rolls Royce is sold by highlighting a fine piece of Faberge jewellery. You see, luxury is used to sell luxury and that is an example of association; one luxury will (help) to sell another. The implications are that only a privileged few of the readers of the display can afford the wares. It is hardly worth trying to sell a genuine blue period Picasso painting without a narrative that speaks of real wealth. The aim of the display is to attract a wealthy purchaser and that desires special treatment.

PEACE AND TRANQUILITY- Again, this is a theme that means so many different things to individuals. These include a quiet week-end break, a peaceful holiday at the seaside or in the countryside, a quiet really rural country hotel, just a simple tranquil rest in one`s own garden...the list is endless. It will be realised that this theme gives ample opportunities for the draftsman to play on the escape from the tempo of everyday life.

Having lulled the reader into the false sense of the well-being to come the advertiser has before him a physical wreck. He has the panacea. So, buy and smoke one of our cigarettes in a quiet wooden glen, woo your girlfriend amidst the swaying golden cornfields - in one of soft sexy sweaters that you are about to buy, float to paradise with your body peacefully reposing on one of our beds...to attain those and other peaceful situations is everyone`s dream and provides ample material for popular and enticing drafts. Peace and tranquillity can so easily be used to lull the reader into buying all those goods and services that will bring...peace and tranquillity.

HUMOUR AND COMEDY - Being humorous is an element in much advertising. It is a state of mind. Being out of humour means being in a bad and/or gloomy mood, not a state of mind that is receptive to the advertiser`s message. All draftsmen must get the reader into a humorous mood. Not, of course, in the sense that he is laughing out loud; but in the sense that he is in a generally contented state. The message must not be cold or analytical; it should be friendly, almost every day. You see, a light-hearted message is more likely to win hearts than a heavy one dripping in meaning. Remember that a draftsman is nearly always composing for the masses - the man-in-the-street and not for a selected few; certainly not for the intelligentsia. This has been previously stated and is repeated as the draftsman must keep well to the fore his likely readership.

If comedy is used it must be closely related to the advertised product. Otherwise, the joke is likely to steal the show and push the product into the background. Comedy must be used very carefully.

Retain in your memory bank the four elements of good advertising **BEING ORIGINAL, BRIEF, DESCRIPTIVE AND HONEST.** A negative must now be added to those four positive items. It is this - never make a joke against a competitor and never use comedy to denigrate anyone. It will not stand up in the marketplace and could well backfire. So, it is repeated, when using comedy make sure that it is light comedy and closely related to the advertised product.

With the above fourteen themes to select from you should have little trouble composing ideas. As an exercise - you own a small two-star hotel some two hundred yards from the coast road at a popular seaside resort in West Sussex. Compose two displays - one for the local Tourist Guide which will circulate throughout the UK, and one for the local evening newspaper. Do not forget to put all the good ideas in your Idea Book for future consideration and use.

Although not really a theme subliminal advertising is an interesting concept. It is a complex form of advertising and employs images of which the reader being targeted is not aware. That individual is looking at or listening to something that is clearly understood by him but - and here is the rub - there is a hidden message/form of persuasion that is conditioning his mind to favour whatever the advertiser is selling or wants him to do. Certain aspects of this form of advertising are restricted by law and it is sensible to use an advertising agent who will know what can and cannot be legally done.

15
IDEAS -
THEIR CREATION AND
USE

THE FIRST THOUGHT - Advertisements that produce the best results are based on an original idea and the bolder the idea the better.

It must be admitted that creating new ideas is not an easy undertaking. Neither is putting a new idea into commercial use. When an idea comes into mind it must be nurtured and cultivated until it is ready to go out and do its job in the marketplace. Firstly, it is vital that you must have faith in the idea. If you, the creator, have doubts it is more than likely to be a flop. Secondly, you must consider ways of implementing the idea. Is it suitable for an everyday item or for a rare luxury one? Is it suitable for a local, regional, national or international display? There are many other questions to be asked and answered within those preceding ones. It is both pointless and profitless having a great idea and misusing it. It is likely that you are a trader and will want to use your new idea to benefit your own business. Although this is understandable you must make sure that the idea is one that fits in with your business. There is little worse than using an idea just because you have created it. If it is not really and truly suitable to use in your business at that point in time do not waste it. Put it in your Idea Book for future consideration and use.

A tip - before use an idea must be considered from all angles and turned over in your mind until you are satisfied that you have squeezed the last drop of sense out of it. That process may give you other ideas and your Ideas Book will soon contain many ideas and suggestions for future displays. Do not forget to consider any negative or bad aspects as they could be the seeds of your future destruction and it may be necessary to eliminate those from future use. You may consider that all that time-consuming examination is excessive - if so, you may like to recall that Oscar Wilde told us that nothing succeeds like excess!

Ideas fly around and come to you at the most inconvenient times. Always, it seems, when not immediately required. It is a sensible plan to capture those ideas as soon as they appear and to retain them for future use. Do not let any idea get away. That is fine advice, but as life goes on ideas that are not used are forgotten. They get lost amongst the thousand and one things and thoughts that everyday keeps one busy. The simple solution is the Ideas Book. Every time that an idea comes to you, be it a good or bad one, jot it down in that book. There will always be a store to dip into when drafting. As ideas help to create other ideas there will forever be an increasing and up-to-date Ideas Book available for you.

Whenever you see or hear of any item that may be of future interest note it in the Ideas Book. If you do not have an Ideas Book start one right now. You will forever be thankful as you pick and choose from its contents - always an idea; never lost for words.

Another book that I have found useful is one listing synonyms - Harrap's English Synonyms is a fantastic book for reference. It enables you to pick an appropriate alternative word for one that you tend to use so often. How many times do you use good, excellent, wonderful or fine? How many times do estate agents use attractive, spacious, sought-after and unique? Too often it seems - they should all buy a Harrap's.

As previously stated new conceptions are hard to come by for the creative gift is possessed by few. Notwithstanding that by radically changing his outlook a reasonably intelligent person can do better than just copy. It takes time and effort to acquire the knack of "grabbing ideas out of the blue", but success follows success once the right road is taken. Creativity involves an attitude of mind. Thoughts must be directed away from the obvious so as to present an idea in a brand new light. As an exercise, take any advertisement out of the local newspaper and rewrite it in as many ways as possible. You will be surprised at the number of different approaches which spring to mind. Each new one will lead to yet another. Like perpetual motion once it is started it is hard to stop. The mind, like the body, when exercised gains new life and strength. As Valentine said in The Two Gentlemen of Verona, "How use doth breed a habit in man". Shakespeare has once again provided the draftsman with some sound advice.

Learn from the skill of successful advertisers. Estate agents, car retailers, supermarkets and so on rely on publicity to earn their corn and have years of experience behind them - all gained in the hard world of real tough business. They are the undisputed masters, all the way from the local newspaper displays to the glossy publicity displays in the top market magazines. Make a regular habit of studying all their work. That will not be time misspent. Place yourself in the draftsman`s shoes and consider the themes and ideas used. Do not copy from what you read - learn from it, meditate over each idea, look at it from different viewpoints and your own ideas will soon emerge. You will soon be aware that ideas grow from ideas not out of antiquated and tedious reiteration. You will realise that many displays that you read will be every day and tired. Do not despair those will teach you all the pitfalls and you will soon get to know which blunders and clangers to avoid.

More often than not an idea comes out of a theme - perhaps from one of the fourteen themes listed in the last chapter. The draftsman selects from the theme one significant and interesting feature which he handles in such a way that it becomes more important than the theme itself. It becomes the attraction. Consider this example, the makers of a world famous computer compares its super perfection with an object that no manufacturer can possibly compete with - the human brain. The reader`s mind latches on to all the facilities possessed by the human brain, he wonders at its sheer complexities and comes to the conclusion that the advertised computer must be the most superior one in the world. It is as wonderful as the human brain. Gosh! The theme is of perfection and the reader`s thoughts are directed to the perfection of the human brain and associates it with the computer. So, such a fine computer must be purchased.

A really good new slant on a subject will make a display that has strong pulling powers. Most people adore anything new; it becomes a talking point and that in itself is a bonus to the advertised.

Do not be downhearted, keep plugging away and sure enough sensible new ideas and adaptations of the best old ideas will soon help you prepare your displays. Always remember - keep in touch with customers and potential ones and listen to their views so that your displays and wares reflect their sentiments and views.

IDEAS IN ACTION

Ideas have to be activated in order to perform their proper functions in the marketplace. I was asked to draft an advertisement for the sale of a penthouse which was luxury personified. It possessed every conceivable up-to-date amenity, exquisite decorations, fantastic panoramic sea and country views and so on. By putting together the adjectives I have used, plus a few more, it was easy to compose an honest and quite descriptive display, but so full of words used every day by many estate agents. The response to that display could well have been "...just another over-priced and over-praised property". Those sentiments are not meant to suggest that I am running down estate agents` advertisements, far from it. I am endeavouring to show that there are other ways of advertising than displaying a mass of over hyped adjectives that we all use every day.

After some cogitation an idea came to the fore - the location, the accommodation...idea for large scale entertaining; the overall conception was generally a little flashy and yet screaming aloud that it was one of the most expensive and luxurious properties on that coast...and the price! It would be an ideal home for a super rich buyer from a top rock band or a top flight international footballer. This was my idea in rough draft. The message was simple and it sold!

UP IN THE CLOUDS
ONLY FIT FOR A SUPER STAR

<u>A PENTHOUSE WITH A VIEW</u>

WHEN YOU INSPECT YOU WILL REALISE THAT SUPERLATIVES FADE INTO INSIGNIFICANCE

(Brief note on location, accommodation and price)

A FINAL WARNING

This final warning is that you must get out of your mind that advertising is "a dry old boring business". If you do not do that you are bound to fail. Advertising is buying an item that you require, selling an item to obtain much needed cash or suggesting to the public what should or should not be done. **TO SUCESSFULLY UNDERTAKE THOSE OBJECTIVES YOU MUST BE ENTHUSIASTIC, DEVOTED TO THE TASK, KEEN TO BEAT ALL COMPETITORS AND EAGER TO SUCCEED.** Unless you regard advertising as being an exciting exercise and truly productive you will not achieve your maximum potential. So, never forget as you work and compose your drafts that creating successful and lucrative displays is fun

THE VERY LAST THOUGHT

The giraffe wanted the most succulent leaves at the top of the tree

Over many centuries by constantly striving to reach his target he succeeded by the gradual and yet persistent stretching of his neck

YOUR PROGRESS WILL BE SO MUCH QUICKER KEEP TRYING AND YOU WILL SUCCEED

**

www.ingramcontent.com/pod-product-compliance
Lightning Source LLC
Chambersburg PA
CBHW051806170526
45167CB00005B/1898

* 9 7 8 1 4 9 6 0 4 2 7 5 0 *